Project Management Institute

MANAGING CHANGE IN ORGANIZATIONS:
A PRACTICE GUIDE

Library of Congress Control Number: 2013946442

ISBN: 978-1-62825-015-2

Published by:
 Project Management Institute, Inc.
 14 Campus Boulevard
 Newtown Square, Pennsylvania 19073-3299 USA
 Phone: +610-356-4600
 Fax: +610-356-4647
 Email: customercare@pmi.org
 Internet: www.PMI.org

PMI Publications welcomes corrections and comments on its books. Please feel free to send comments on typographical, formatting, or other errors. Simply make a copy of the relevant page of the book, mark the error, and send it to: Book Editor, PMI Publications, 14 Campus Boulevard, Newtown Square, PA 19073-3299 USA.

To inquire about discounts for resale or educational purposes, please contact the PMI Book Service Center.
 PMI Book Service Center
 P.O. Box 932683, Atlanta, GA 31193-2683 USA
 Phone: 1-866-276-4764 (within the U.S. or Canada) or +1-770-280-4129 (globally)
 Fax: +1-770-280-4113
 Email: info@bookorders.pmi.org

The paper used in this book complies with the Permanent Paper Standard issued by the National Information Standards Organization (Z39.48—1984).

10 9 8 7 6 5 4 3 2 1

NOTICE

The Project Management Institute, Inc. (PMI) standards and guideline publications, of which the document contained herein is one, are developed through a voluntary consensus standards development process. This process brings together volunteers and/or seeks out the views of persons who have an interest in the topic covered by this publication. While PMI administers the process and establishes rules to promote fairness in the development of consensus, it does not write the document and it does not independently test, evaluate, or verify the accuracy or completeness of any information or the soundness of any judgments contained in its standards and guideline publications.

PMI disclaims liability for any personal injury, property or other damages of any nature whatsoever, whether special, indirect, consequential or compensatory, directly or indirectly resulting from the publication, use of application, or reliance on this document. PMI disclaims and makes no guaranty or warranty, expressed or implied, as to the accuracy or completeness of any information published herein, and disclaims and makes no warranty that the information in this document will fulfill any of your particular purposes or needs. PMI does not undertake to guarantee the performance of any individual manufacturer or seller's products or services by virtue of this standard or guide.

In publishing and making this document available, PMI is not undertaking to render professional or other services for or on behalf of any person or entity, nor is PMI undertaking to perform any duty owed by any person or entity to someone else. Anyone using this document should rely on his or her own independent judgment or, as appropriate, seek the advice of a competent professional in determining the exercise of reasonable care in any given circumstances. Information and other standards on the topic covered by this publication may be available from other sources, which the user may wish to consult for additional views or information not covered by this publication.

PMI has no power, nor does it undertake to police or enforce compliance with the contents of this document. PMI does not certify, test, or inspect products, designs, or installations for safety or health purposes. Any certification or other statement of compliance with any health or safety-related information in this document shall not be attributable to PMI and is solely the responsibility of the certifier or maker of the statement.

TABLE OF CONTENTS

LIST OF TABLE AND FIGURES

PREFACE

Managing Change in Organizations: A Practice Guide is a complementary document to PMI's foundational standards. This practice guide provides guidance on implementing change management across the Knowledge Areas and associated processes in the foundational standards. This practice guide exemplifies PMI's continuing commitment to support the project management profession with a defined body of knowledge.

PMI views change management as an essential capability that cascades across and throughout portfolio, program, and project management. PMI believes that all strategic change in organizations is delivered through programs and projects. Successful organizations lead change by managing their projects and programs effectively.

Change management is addressed in *A Guide to the Project Management Body of Knowledge (PMBOK® Guide); The Standard for Program Management; The Standard for Portfolio Management;* and *Organizational Project Management Maturity Model (OPM3®).* From stakeholder management to communications to human resources management, elements of change management appear throughout PMI's foundational standards but are not specifically identified as the phrase "change management."

A practice guide is a new category in the PMI library of standards, which is intended to encourage discussion related to areas of practice where there may not yet be consensus about what constitutes good practice. Innovation combined with a dynamic external environment drives organizations and practitioners to act more quickly and become more adaptive to manage uncertainty; therefore, PMI introduced this practice guide to identify how adaptive approaches integrate with PMI's foundational standards.

Practice guides are developed by leading experts in the field using a new process that provides reliable information and reduces the time required for development and distribution. PMI defines a practice guide as a standards product that provides supporting supplemental information and instructions for the application of PMI standards. Practice guides are not consensus-based standards and do not go through the full exposure draft process. However, the resulting work may be introduced later as a potential standard and, if so, will then be subjected to PMI's documented process for the development of full consensus standards.

1

INTRODUCTION

1.1 The Purpose of this Practice Guide

Executives in today's world are aware of the changing business environment, and that the rate of change is increasing, driven by such factors as the exponential growth and global availability of information, technologies, technology-based infrastructure, and the expanding global marketplace that these factors facilitate. Executives appreciate how important it is to have clear and powerful strategies to guide their organizational development, including a means of executing those strategies reliably and effectively.

Executing strategy well requires the successful delivery of change programs: programs to improve performance and implement innovations. Such programs, however, have typically not been executed well. An article in *Harvard Business Review* noted that the performance improvement efforts of many companies have little impact on operational and financial results [1].[1]

Experience in the last two decades has demonstrated that it doesn't have to be that way, and both the project management community and the change management community have devoted considerable efforts in addressing this issue. For example, PMI's 2012 *Pulse of the Profession*™ *In-Depth Report: Organizational Agility* [2] concluded organizations achieving higher-than-average success rates from their portfolio of programs and projects have not only increased their use of standardized portfolio, program, and project practices, but have adopted, among other things, rigorous change management to better adapt to shifting market conditions.

Rigorous change management practices are essential for a standardized organizational project management practice as this practice guide demonstrates. Organizational project management (OPM) is defined as the systematic management of portfolios, programs, and projects in alignment with the organization's strategic business goals, so as to ensure that the organization undertakes the right projects, allocates resources appropriately, and appreciates the relationships among strategic vision, the initiatives that support the vision, and their objectives and deliverables.

Regardless of the extent or maturity of OPM in an organization, this practice guide describes how portfolio, program, and project management needs to increase the effective practice of change management inherent in the PMI foundational standards so that strategy can be executed reliably and effectively. It provides practical help to executives and managers who are charged with the responsibility for making change happen in and through programs and projects. It sets the practices, processes, and disciplines on managing change in the context of portfolio, program, and project management, and illustrates how change management is an essential ingredient in using project management as the vehicle for delivering organizational strategy.

---

[1] The numbers in brackets refer to the list of references at the end of this practice guide.

In order to get the most from this practice guide, it is important to understand what it does not cover.

- This practice guide does not advise organizations on how to develop or craft strategy.

- This practice guide does not cover the individual and organizational psychology of change—that is the professional domain of the organizational psychologist and organizational development specialist. This practice guide does not make recommendations about improving organizational performance through business process reengineering—that is the domain of organizational development theory and practice for business process improvement.

- This practice guide does not contain detailed descriptions of the processes and practices of project management—these are detailed elsewhere in PMI's four foundational standards (*A Guide to the Project Management Body of Knowledge* – Fifth Edition [3], *The Standard for Program Management* – Third Edition [4], *The Standard for Portfolio Management* – Third Edition [5], *Organizational Project Management Maturity Model* – Third Edition [6].

- This practice guide does not provide advice to program and project managers about how to control changes to project scope or to project plans. These activities are covered in PMI's foundational standards where they are presented as "change control."

This practice guide brings together two sets of ideas and discussions that have tended to develop in rather separate domains: (1) change management in the realm of organizational development and human resource management; and (2) portfolio, program, and project management in projectized organizations. In bringing these two sets of ideas together, this practice guide provides executives and managers in the project community with a guide on how to improve change management practice within portfolio, program and project management. It also provides practitioners from disciplines such as organizational development or human resource management with insights into how project management provides the context and the vehicle for delivering change.

Managing portfolios, programs, and projects is an integrative job, and managing change in organizations requires the integration of many functions and professional disciplines. This practice guide provides a framework for integration that is entirely consistent with the principles, practices, and processes of project management. It provides practical wisdom to a wide audience.

1.2 The Need for this Guide

Recent research supported by PMI [7] has shown that projects for changing the organization or for improving its ability to accomplish its purpose occur in virtually every organization and represent the fourth most common type of project undertaken. In view of this, it is surprising that only one in five organizations formally adopt organizational change management practices. Combined with the findings of the 2012 *Pulse of the Profession*™ report [8] where organizations reporting higher-than-average success rates for projects also report higher-than-average adoption of organizational change management practices, it is clear that this practice guide meets a real need (stop wasting money and other resources on failed projects) and presents an opportunity (respond to a changing commercial and technical environment).

1

Change is present to some extent in all market sectors, although markets such as automotive, IT, telecom, and utilities report above-average susceptibility to change. Nevertheless, not all market sectors show the same degree of readiness to adopt formal organizational change management. For financial and business services organizations, business change is not only a characteristic of many of the projects undertaken in the sector, it is also one of the strategic drivers of performance. Poorly implemented change programs lose customers and attract unwelcome negative media attention. In the government sector, business change projects represent a high proportion of all projects, and business change ranks very highly as a strategic driver. For these organizations, this practice guide deals with practices and processes that are central and of vital importance for success.

There are organizations in other market sectors that excel in managing projects for clients but are deficient in their ability to change or improve their own capabilities or to respond to changing market conditions. For executives and managers in these organizations, this practice guide presents an opportunity to transition an existing strength in one part of the organization to other areas where it is currently lacking.

1.3 The Intended Audience

This practice guide will be of value to any executive or manager who is involved in the oversight, design, management, or appraisal of portfolios, programs, or projects and their inherent change impact.

This practice guide is intended for:

- Executives in functions such as organizational development or human resources;
- Executives with responsibility for business divisions or business units;
- Executives or managers involved in the support of organizational project management, such as those responsible for PMOs or Centers of Excellence;
- Executives or managers involved in the management or oversight of portfolios or programs;
- Program managers;
- Project managers;
- Organizational development professionals who are involved with the design and implementation of business improvement programs or projects.

1.4 Overview of the Guide

The practice guide is organized in a logical fashion so the user is able to quickly locate the section(s) of particular interest. It is not written necessarily to be read in its entirety, but rather to allow users to focus on the specific sections that are of greatest interest. Some information is repeated in one or more sections, in order that each individual section can be understood.

1.4.1 Section 2

Section 2 briefly reviews the essence of change management as it is described in the literature. It explains the need for purposeful and dynamic implementation of strategies to transform the organization in response to changing external circumstances. As the world becomes more turbulent, complex, and ambiguous, there is a greater need for an organizational capability to address change. Organizations need to be agile when responding to rapidly changing conditions.

A framework for achieving agility is introduced, which is consistent with the extensive study of organizational change that has taken place during the past two or three decades and also with the proven processes of portfolio, program, and project management described in PMI's foundational standards. The benefits of creating culture with the agility to influence the beneficial effect of change are considered, and the need for change leadership at multiple levels in the organization is emphasized.

Salient characteristics of the nature and process of change are reviewed, considering it from (a) different perspectives such as the impact of change on people and the different ways in which different groups of stakeholders interact to make sense of what is happening to them; (b) the processes of embedding change in organizations; and (c) different "orders" of change, when considered from a systems point of view. How the different elements of the "change life cycle" framework reflect the principles of change from the different perspectives are reviewed, and factors critical to applying the framework successfully are identified.

1.4.2 Section 3

Section 3 proposes how the function of change management can be implemented effectively in an organization that has created (or is creating) an organization-wide approach to the management of programs, projects, and portfolios of programs and projects.

The value of change management is discussed in terms of aligning programs and projects with organizational strategy and also of transitioning project results into operations to realize the intended benefits. This section describes how the intensity of change management practices varies at different stages of the life cycle of portfolios, programs, projects, and operations, and covers the important topic of assessing an organization's readiness for change.

Finally, those elements of change management that are critical to the successful application of portfolio, program, and project management are reviewed, and common causes of failure are analyzed.

1.4.3 Section 4

Section 4 examines change management as a function of managing portfolios of programs and projects—an important and complex task involving many different roles and functions and prompting strong emotional feelings of attachment to particular initiatives on the part of senior managers.

The ten underlying principles and practices of portfolio management contained in *The Standard for Portfolio Management* – Third Edition are described, and the explicit considerations involved in change management are developed for the Defining, Aligning, and Authorizing and Controlling Portfolio Process Groups.

Guidance is provided for conducting an impact assessment to ascertain the extent to which the organization is positioned to accommodate the change impact implicit in a specific strategic initiative.

1.4.4 Section 5

Section 5 covers program management and considers change management practices and issues in this increasingly important context.

The nature and purpose of program management is considered, with reference to *The Standard for Program Management* – Third Edition, and components of the life cycle for programs are compared with corresponding components of the change life cycle framework introduced in Section 2. Specific topics, such as clarifying the need for change when the program is expected to deliver anticipated benefits, planning stakeholder engagement, preparing the organization for change, and measuring the adoption rate throughout the organization and the subsequent delivery of benefits, are described in a way that exhibits the change elements within program management concepts. Section 5 describes how to integrate and sustain change within the organization and summarizes change management capabilities that need to be developed for program management to be effective.

1.4.5 Section 6

Section 6 provides information on how change management impacts the management and outcomes of projects and which change management activities are indispensable to the effective management of projects. Guidance is provided to project managers on which aspects of change management should be considered when managing a project, depending upon the characteristics, scope, and impact of the project, and when applicable, its relationship to program management. This section also provides guidance to project managers regarding the essential nature of project management and highlights specific change management activities for each of the five Project Management Process Groups and applicable Knowledge Areas described in *A Guide to the Project Management Body of Knowledge (PMBOK® Guide)* – Fifth Edition.

1.5 Summary

Managing Change in Organizations: A Practice Guide combines the cumulative wisdom of the change management community with the process and practice standards of the project management community. This practice guide is an invaluable aid to any executive or manager seeking to change an organization by executing strategy through delivering portfolios, programs, or projects.

2

WHAT IS CHANGE MANAGEMENT?

2.1 Overview

Change management is a comprehensive, cyclic, and structured approach for transitioning individuals, groups, and organizations from a current state to a future state with intended business benefits. It helps organizations to integrate and align people, processes, structures, culture, and strategy. Successful organizations do not evolve randomly, but through purposeful and dynamic strategies that anticipate, influence, and respond effectively to emergent and shifting external trends, patterns, and events. Organizations will survive and thrive using a disciplined approach to portfolio, program, and project management and responsive, flexible, and effective change management inherent within that context.

In the current context, portfolio, program, and project leaders need to focus on implementing and integrating change management within the organization's current methodology; this is imperative for organizational success in turbulent and uncertain environments having complex ramifications.

Most organizations have shortened the time horizons for business forecasting and strategic planning due to the business environment's volatility. Although business forecasts for the next 3 to 5 years may not be in alignment, most agree on two facets of the future state:

- The business environment is changing, and the rate of change is accelerating. The exponential growth and global availability of information, technologies, and technology-based infrastructure, as well as the expanding global marketplace, drive this change.

- Accurate, detailed forecasting over a long time horizon is not possible and therefore cannot be used to develop long-term plans to ensure a competitive position in the future. In order for an organization to succeed in the future, it needs to have a robust change process—one that can continuously retune an organization's processes to support the management's vision and react quickly to changes in the business environment.

In order for a robust change process to occur, leaders need to challenge their assumptions and adjust business and leadership models from what has worked in the past to what has become a business imperative for organizational success in a complex environment. While many leaders may dislike change and resist it, the alternative to change may well be obsolescence or irrelevance.

PMI's 2013 *Pulse of the Profession™* [9] states that high-performing organizations focus on execution and alignment by:

- Maturing portfolio management practices to improve the balance between investment and risk,

- Improving organizational agility to allow flexibility and quick response, and

- Tracking benefits realization past the end of a project through operations to verify return on investment.

Executives, practitioners, and stakeholders involved with the changes resulting from a turbulent and uncertain business environment need to develop a firm understanding of the methodologies and flexibilities surrounding changes inherent in the business environment. Figure 2-1 represents a comprehensive framework for change that is introduced in this section and further elaborated in subsequent sections. It encompasses the topic of

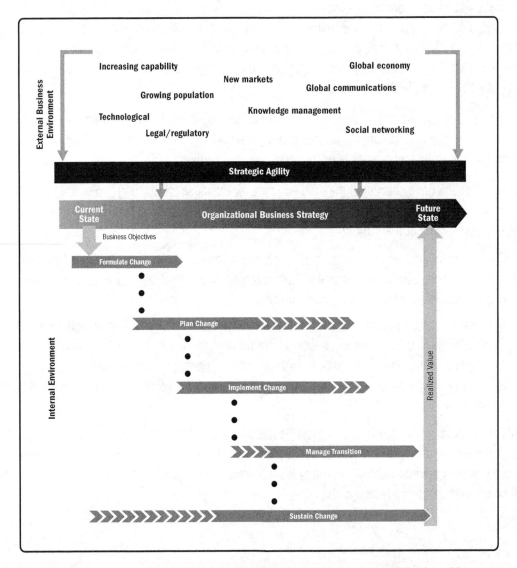

Figure 2-1. Strategic Agility Through Disciplined Portfolio, Program, and Project Management

2

strategic agility that reflects an organization's capability to sense and respond to external or internal threats and opportunities. Strategic agility is defined as the capability of a business to proactively seize and take advantage of business environment changes while demonstrating resilience resulting from unforeseen changes. The change life cycle framework, a subset of this figure, is further described in Section 2.4 and applied to portfolio, program, and project management in subsequent sections of this practice guide.

The challenges facing the project management community are proportionate in difficulty to the increasing complexity and turbulence in today's market environment. Program- and project-related work is becoming more critical to an organization's success. Portfolio, program, and project practitioners are asked to initiate and successfully complete undertakings that are increasingly complicated and interconnected in sometimes subtle and unexpected ways. There is little tolerance for failure. Often resources are not focused on the right priorities or there is a lack of understanding the vision, which is a major reason for program and project failure. In addition, the 2013 *Pulse of the Profession™* indicates that failed projects waste an organization's money.

Paying attention to the embedded change management elements of portfolio, program, and project management substantially increases the likelihood of successful program and project implementation by addressing all aspects of the change (e.g., people, process, systems, structure, etc.).

Research by PMI and other organizations provides evidence of the impact of change through the use of projects and programs. The research also shows the influence of change leadership as a critical element of portfolio, program, and project management success.

2.2 Change as a Strategy

Strategic planning should be an iterative, emergent, and continually evolving process—it can no longer be an annual, top-down process. Organizations need to embrace and adopt change in their strategy to compete and to ensure long-term success. Major change includes innovation, improvement, and relationships with stakeholders. Organizations need to react to change internally with the same intensity as they react to changes in their external environments.

Organizations need to make sense of their business context, develop strategies to adjust quickly, and deliver these strategies effectively through a formalized project management methodology. In short, organizations need to be strategically agile and more effective at delivering change through portfolio, program, and project management.

2.2.1 External Drivers of Change

Survival in a turbulent business climate is a fundamental challenge for all. Competitiveness and success are earned by (a) continually evaluating products and services for the benefit of customers, and (b) rapidly responding to abrupt changes driven by the enterprise environmental factors such as the examples shown in Table 2-1.

Ethics, environmental impact, and social responsibility have been added to the traditional organizational performance criteria of revenue generation and profitability. The continued rise of the digital economy makes

Table 2-1. Environmental Factors Affecting Products and Services

Technological	Cultural	Socioeconomic
Knowledge management	Higher levels of education	Global economy
Computational power	Social networking	Growing population
Increasing capability	Cultural shift	Shifting demographics
Global communications	Social pressures	New markets
		Legal/regulatory

customers more knowledgeable and less forgiving. Transparency makes it harder for organizations to hide mistakes. The era of information-driven globalization is characterized by frequent, rapid, and sometimes unpredictable change. All of these factors increase the speed of change, because change has a rippling effect that can impact and disrupt an organization.

2.2.2 Developing an Agile Culture

The ability to prepare for change is directly related to strategic agility or organizational agility. PMI's 2012 *Pulse of the Profession™ In-Depth Report: Organizational Agility* revealed how organizational agility impacts success and discussed how to increase that agility. Successful organizations are aggressively reshaping their culture and business practices by the following actions:

- Rigorous change management to better adapt to frequently shifting market conditions;
- More collaborative and robust risk management; and
- Increased use of standardized portfolio, program, and project practices.

The report defines criteria that classifies organizations as high or low agility and states that highly agile organizations are twice as likely to see increased success with their new initiatives as their low-agility counterparts.

In addition to having the right technology and core processes, an organization needs to be able to create "change-ready" employees. Portfolio, program, and project management are about change readiness. The 2013 *Pulse of the Profession™* clearly identified that organizations that deliver change effectively use project management training.

However, constant change, whether proactive or reactive, places enormous stress on the organization and its stakeholders. Management needs to help stakeholders recognize that the change process for a specific task will have measurable points of success, yet there is no end to the total business change process.

2.2.3 Sponsoring Change

Effective change management requires enhanced capabilities in the portfolio, program, and project teams. These capabilities should be part of a team's core capabilities; the team needs the functional knowledge and expertise to ensure that the appropriate change management activities are initiated, planned, monitored, executed, and evaluated. In order to effectively manage change in the portfolio, program, and project management domains, an organization may need to incorporate the following functions and activities:

- **Governance Board.** A governance board in the organizational project management (OPM) context provides overall oversight for the portfolio, program, or project change process, setting direction and providing leadership. It also ensures that the change process remains aligned with the organization's strategic vision and direction. A governance board deals with the business issues associated with the change and ensures the achievement of change outcomes/benefits.

- **Sponsor.** A sponsor provides resources required for change and has the ultimate responsibility for the program or project, building commitment for the change particularly at the senior management level across the organization. Direct responsibility and accountability for the change needs to be clearly defined and accepted at an appropriately high level within an organization. Consequently, the sponsor for a change effort should be someone who has sufficient authority, influence, power, enthusiasm, and time to ensure that any conflicts that could impede the change are resolved in a timely and appropriate fashion.

  PMI's 2013 *Pulse of the Profession™* directly links success with an active sponsor who exhibits visible sponsorship and advocacy for the change effort, assesses and mitigates any resistance to the change, and oversees the business and management issues that surface.

  The sponsor's active and visible support of the change from initiation to completion is important to deal with the organization's internal politics, to ensure that stakeholders are represented and continue to actively support the change throughout the process, and to build alliances with others across the organization to ensure a successful outcome.

- **Leads.** The lead function, which may be spread across multiple individuals, supports the overall change management process and implementation, including coordination of associated work streams within the scope of the project. The lead ensures that the change management process addresses the impact of requirements on business processes, workforce, and infrastructure, and monitors the implementation and risks. The lead also coordinates communications relating to the change to all relevant stakeholders through the appropriate channels. The lead may escalate change-related issues through the project manager for discussion and decision to the governance board or sponsor.

- **Integrators.** The integrator function is responsible for preparation and integration of the change into the business and therefore has a major role in its implementation. Integrators ensure that routine business activities are performed at an acceptable level during the change. Integrators may break down wide-ranging or complex change initiatives into groups of activities by business area. The function of the integrators is to ensure that diverse work processes remain aligned to the overall objectives. Integrators may be functional managers, executives, or other individuals, depending upon the nature of the change.

- **Agents.** Agents are active proponents and drivers of the change. Agents may be early adopters who see the business benefits of the change and have embraced it. Agents come from every area of the business and all levels of the organization. Once identified, agents become a resource for integrating the change in their respective environments, thereby driving the change into the organization.

- **Recipients.** Recipients may be people directly or indirectly impacted by a change. Recipients collectively are considered as one of the many stakeholder groups, and their input into the change process is critical.

Sensemaking activities (the conversational and social practices that enable individuals and groups to make sense of what is happening around them) are usually directed at the recipients to help them make the change transition. A focus on sensemaking does create and build on a deep understanding of the situation. It is the information that is received, combined with what individuals, small groups, organizations, and cultures bring to the situation, which includes prior knowledge and belief systems. Active and targeted communications are essential elements to gain the recipients' support. Recipients require attention and monitoring as the change initiative progresses because they may foster or hinder the integration of the change and its sustained success.

2.3 The Nature and Process of Change

Much research has been done with respect to the human dynamic of change. This research has led to numerous theories of how people respond to change and the various models used to plan successful change processes.

Most people deal with change-related stress and anxiety by trying to maintain a sense of control over their lives. This feeling of control is achieved when people believe that they can make sense of what will happen to them and that they can influence the outcome of events. Recipients' perception is affected by many factors and will impact the process of sensemaking.

A change process tests both the human aspect and project management's need for control and requires the capability to deal with ambiguity.

Portfolio managers typically work in a relatively stable, but ambiguous context as they need to assess many organizational initiatives (programs, projects, and other activities) on an ongoing basis against a medium-term corporate strategy. Program managers work in a complex and turbulent context where change is the norm; they have to be agile and tolerant to both ambiguity and uncertainty. Both portfolio and program managers have to deal with change on a daily basis. Project managers control key parameters, such as milestones, resources, dependencies of tasks, and task assignments. Project managers typically feel in control when they are able to capture all of the technical aspects and events in a well-developed project plan. However, after a meeting with a sponsor, governance board, or clients, project managers may be surprised to find that confusion exists regarding the plans. Project management tools such as change control processes for adjusting scope or requirements are not sufficient to address the types of changes needed.

2.3.1 Common Models of Change

Change originates from external sources through technological advances and demographic changes and socioeconomic pressures. Change also originates from inside the organization, possibly as a management response to issues such as changing client needs, costs, human resources, or performance issues. Change may affect one area or the entire organization. Nevertheless, all change, whether from internal or external sources, large or small, involves adopting new mindsets, processes, policies, practices, and behavior.

2

To manage a change successfully requires a structured approach as well as the ability to deal with emergent situations. A number of change management models have been designed to help manage the change component successfully. Most change models and theories share a number of characteristics.

- All models identify a process in which the organization establishes a reason and need for the change. This step begins with the leaders of the organization. The challenge for organizational leaders is to create an atmosphere where people are engaged and motivated to achieve expectations.

- All models incorporate the development of a vision or desired business result and movement from the current state to a future state. Visioning is one of the most important steps of a change process. People often resist change unless there is an evident and well-communicated benefit to the change; vision helps people in the organization understand where they are going. When there is a difference between the stated vision and reality, it leads to confusion and a loss of trust that can result in failure.

- Some models address the concept of changing or creating organizational processes to deliver change. This step evaluates the current systems, processes, and capabilities to facilitate change.

- All models incorporate the idea of incremental progress by reinforcing and creating small improvements to encourage additional change. Most organizations have a model for improvement. One of the most common is the plan-do-check-act (PDCA) cycle defined by Shewhart and modified by Deming.

- All models address the importance of communications in order to gain support for the change and to encourage buy-in. Successful organizations acquire, integrate, and use new knowledge to be successful. Organizations need to combine and exchange knowledge assets in order to enhance processes and guard against failure. Understanding where an organization is and where they should be is part of this process.

As a means of understanding the similarities and differences in the various models, a brief description of some of the well-known models in each category is provided in Sections 2.3.1.1 through 2.3.1.4.

2.3.1.1 Category 1—Change as a Psychological Transition

The Bridges' Transition Model provides a good understanding of what occurs to individuals psychologically when an organizational change takes place. This model differentiates between change and transition. Change is situational and happens whether or not people transition through it. Transition is a psychological process where people gradually accept the details of the new situation and the changes that come with it.

Change typically involves turbulence and disruption of the status quo. It is often referred to as the "change curve" and is based on a model originally developed in the 1960s by Elisabeth Kubler-Ross to explain the grieving process that a terminally ill patient progresses through when informed of an illness. The change curve is represented graphically as a form of a U or V with time on the X-axis and stakeholder emotional reaction on the Y-axis to reflect the psychological stages stakeholders go through when a change is announced and implemented. Some stakeholders respond with stress and negative emotions when a change is announced. Sponsors and portfolio, program, and project managers need to understand the implications of the stages represented by the change curve on the change implementation process. By the 1980s, the change curve was a firm fixture in change management circles. The curve and its associated emotions can be used to predict how performance is likely to be affected by the announcement and subsequent implementation of a significant change.

2.3.1.2 Category 2—Change as a Process

John Kotter's eight steps to transforming organizations are based upon the analysis of 100 different organizations going through change. This research highlighted eight key lessons, which were converted into an eight-step model. Kotter's change model is often referred to as a top-down approach to change where the need for and approach to change originates at the top levels of the organization and then is promoted down through the organization's layers of management to the change recipients.

2.3.1.3 Category 3—Change Represented as Systems Models

Continuous improvement is an essential survival strategy for every organization in order to be able to adjust to higher standards and changing conditions. There is a foundational tenet that should be addressed as an organization's managers attempt to implement organizational project management: Orders of Change.

In 1974, Watzlawick, Weakland, and Fisch [10] surmised that most of the existing theories of change were philosophical and had been derived from mathematics and physics. These theories explained what they called first-order and second-order changes:

- A first-order change is usually described as a change in the manner in which processes and procedures are performed in an organization. It is considered to be an adjustment within the existing system of the organization. An example of a first-order change is a new status report that all project managers are expected to use. Figure 2-2 shows no substantial change to the organization when a first-order change

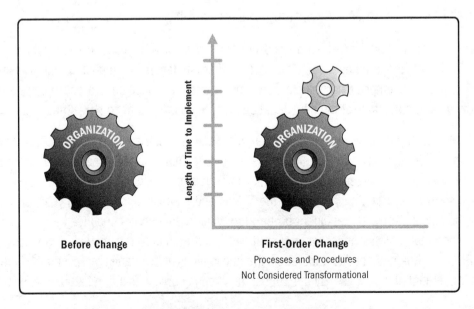

Figure 2-2. First-Order Change

is applied. A first-order change is reversible and is not considered to be a transformational change. People are usually not threatened by a first-order change because their fundamental competencies are not being challenged.

- A second-order change is significantly different from a first-order change. A second-order change is transformational and irreversible in nature; once started there is usually no way to revert back to the old way of doing things (see Figure 2-3). It usually requires new learning for employees or a new way of seeing things.

This type of change usually occurs as the result of a strategic change or a major crisis such as a threat against the organization's survival. Second-order change redefines the way work is conducted or introduces a new concept for the organization. An example of a second-order change is an organization that adopts program management for the first time. This requires a business focus in how work is approached. It also means that, for the first time, the organization will be projecting benefits, managing benefits, and realizing benefits. This type of change requires new policies, new focus, new processes, new training, and possibly a more robust accountability hierarchy that drives real accountability.

A second-order change may be threatening to people. New ways of doing work threaten competencies (Will I be able to perform the new job?) and the individual's results (Will they find out I'm not good enough?).

In 2000, Casey [11] theorized that there was another level of change—a third-order. This third-order change requires a change in values. Whereas a second-order change is based on a redefinition or a new concept, a third-order change modifies the founding principles of the organization.

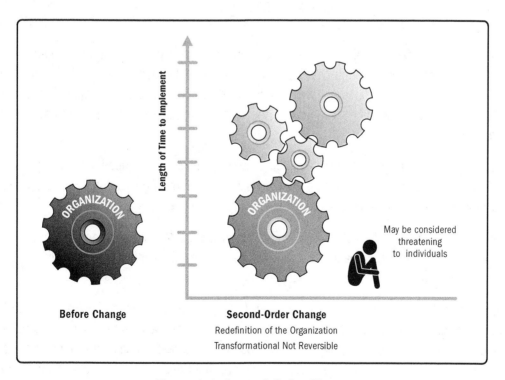

Figure 2-3. Second-Order Change

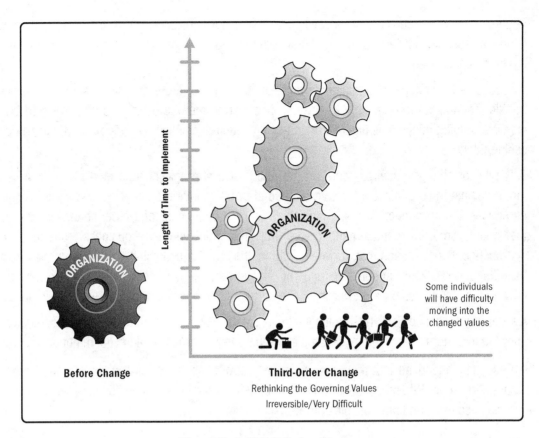

Figure 2-4. Third-Order Change

An example of a third-order change is when an organization's leaders take pride in their organizational ability to get things done quickly and their belief that they do not need process. The leaders then realize they have embedded a process into the daily work that does not work. They decide to change the philosophy of the organization to process improvement (i.e., embracing Six Sigma for the first time) and begin the transformation to a culture of process improvement.

This is the most difficult type of change to facilitate in an organization. It requires understanding the behaviors, thoughts, and feelings of people. Many people who work in a free-form organization may have difficulty moving into a process improvement culture, as depicted in Figure 2-4.

When comparing the three orders of change, as shown in Table 2-2, note that the recipient of what is being changed differs in each category of change. With the differences in the recipient, the difficulty increases and the time to facilitate and sustain the change lengthens.

The change life cycle framework presented in Section 2.4 depicts a logical sequence of integrative steps to help plan and execute portfolios, programs, and projects with second- and third-order change objectives. The magnitude and extent of work applied to the initiative needs to be gauged. Some simple initiatives may require all steps of the change process, but not to any substantial depth. Other initiatives will require all steps of the model, and within each step, substantial work needs to be completed in order to facilitate and sustain the change.

Table 2-2. Comparing Orders of Change

Category of Change	Recipient	Difficulty	Length of Initiative	Reversibility
First-order change	Procedures—modifications in how work is done	minor	short	easily reversed
Second-order change	Policies—doing something significantly different	moderate	medium	irreversible
Third-order change	Values—rethinking the governing values	very	long	irreversible

2.3.1.4 Category 4—Custom Change Models

Systematic and disciplined structures for managing change have often been customized for an organization to meet its specific needs. Two examples of customized change models are:

- American Express developed a change process consisting of major change phases with key issues that were addressed in each phase:

  o Scope the change.

  o Create a vision.

  o Drive commitment.

  o Accelerate the transition.

  o Sustain momentum.

- Jack Welch, former CEO of General Electric, introduced a change management model that has since become a change blueprint for many organizations. The model contains six straightforward steps:

  o Clear expression of the reasons for change, articulating the "why" before getting to the "how."

  o Establish the vision for the new state of affairs and outline what the change will achieve.

  o Provide strong leadership and obtain support from the most senior organizational level.

  o Mobilize the workforce by engaging staff in the planning and definition of the new process.

  o Measure success and analyze outcomes using solid metrics.

  o Maintain consistency.

2.3.1.5 Summary of Models

As illustrated, there are many different models and theories of change. A change model or framework helps to ensure that most aspects of the proposed change are considered. The change life cycle framework for a portfolio, program, and project management environment is described in Section 2.4.

Change management is the process of taking a planned and structured approach to align an organization with the change. In its simplest and most effective form, change management involves working with an organization's stakeholder groups to help them understand what the change means for them, make and sustain the transition, and overcome any challenges. From a management perspective, this pertains to the organizational and behavioral adjustments that need to be made to accommodate and sustain the change. Change models can help structure these processes.

The general guidelines for an effective change management process in the change life cycle framework for portfolio, program, and project management are:

- **Formulating the change** by identifying and clarifying the need for change, assessing readiness for change, and delineating the scope of change.

- **Planning the change** by defining the change approach and planning stakeholder engagement as well as transition and integration.

- **Implementing the change** by preparing the organization for change, mobilizing the stakeholders, and delivering project outputs.

- **Managing the change transition** by transitioning the outputs into business operations, measuring the adoption rate and the change outcomes and benefits, and adjusting the plan to address discrepancies.

- **Sustaining the change** on an ongoing basis through communication, consultation, and representation of the stakeholders; conducting sensemaking activities; and measuring benefits realization.

2.3.2 Corporate Culture and Change

When an organization identifies the type of change needed and chooses a change process, the next step is to understand the culture and political environment in which the change will occur. There are two aspects concerning the relationship between culture and change: (1) Build on the existing culture when implementing change; and (2) Determine how to transition towards a transformed culture. Both require effective leadership.

Culture is generally thought of as "the way we do things around here." Culture involves an explicit way of working (the formal systems and processes in place and how they operate) and a tacit level of operation (the informal and semiformal networks and other activities people employ to get things done and bypass, subvert, or seek to influence the more formal processes).

When dealing with change it is important to recognize that different organizations have different cultures and that within organizations, different areas have their own way of doing things or their own subcultures. Culture is the frame of reference that helps distinguish one group of people from another and establishes a unique set of formal and informal ground rules for opinions and behavior. Some organization leaders believe that changing their culture is a "quick fix." In reality, it is essential for an organization's survival, but it is not quick in any way.

The following characteristics are crucial for understanding the relationship between culture and the success of a change process:

- Culture is composed of the prevailing beliefs, behaviors, and assumptions of an organization. These serve as a guide to what are considered appropriate or inappropriate behaviors of individuals and groups.

- Culture is shared. It provides cohesion throughout an organization and across organizational functional boundaries.

- Culture is developed over time. An organization's culture is the product of beliefs, current behaviors, past practices, and assumptions that have contributed to its success.

- Culture is nurtured in a self-fulfilling cycle. Culture provides a means of understanding strategic decisions, which allows expectations to develop. Expectations generate thoughts and emotions, which lead to decisions about implementation of changes in the organization. Those decisions guide and justify activities that are supportive of the culture.

- Culture needs to be assessed when thinking of implementing major change to see if it aligns to better enable success of the change. A culture that is at odds with the change will prevent successful implementation and the change should be seriously reevaluated before significant investments are made in time, human resources and budget. For example the transformation of IBM from a computer manufacturer to a service organization required significant cultural change.

- A key element to enhancing success and minimizing the chance of dysfunctional behavior is the degree to which the portfolio, program, or project manager can actively influence the culture to support the change by:

  o Assessing stakeholder change resistance and/or support for the change and actively addressing any of the gaps,

  o Ensuring clarity of vision and values among stakeholders about the change initiative,

  o Creating understanding among the various stakeholder groups about their individual and interdependent roles in attaining the goal(s) of the change initiative, and

  o Building strong alignment between stakeholder attitudes and strategic goals and objectives.

Whenever a discrepancy exists between the current culture and the objectives of the portfolio, program, or project, the culture generally prevails.

2.4 Introduction to the Change Life Cycle Framework

Figure 2-5, the change life cycle framework, is a concurrent set of subprocesses where multiple activities take place in an ordered but nonsequential way. It is an iterative model where adaptive change occurs on a continual basis in response to evolving circumstances. The change life cycle framework is introduced here and further elaborated as applicable in subsequent sections of this practice guide.

2.4.1 Formulate Change

Formulate change by translating an organization's strategic plan into tangible objectives that are aligned with stakeholders' needs and expectations.

- **Identify/clarify need for change.** Establish the need for change and the contribution needed for continued growth and sustainable competitive advantage.

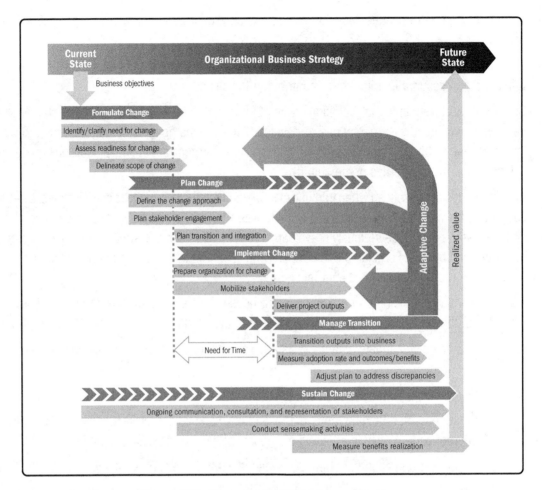

Figure 2-5. Change Life Cycle Framework

- **Assess readiness for change.** Assess the change readiness of organizational systems, structures, culture, and people that are impacted by or needed for the change.

- **Delineate scope of change.** Clarify expected outcomes of the change and define the extent and activities necessary for successful change.

2.4.2 Plan Change

Plan for change by including both the "what" and "how" of change so that people, process, technology, structure, and cultural issues are all integrated into the overall portfolio, program, or project plan. A seamless integration of the change plan (how) with the portfolio, program, or project plans (what) is essential so that only one plan exists.

- **Define the change approach.** Align the change approach with the culture of the organization.

- **Plan stakeholder engagement.** Identify and engage all stakeholders, internal and external, affected by or interested in the outcomes and plan for their ongoing involvement.

- **Plan transition and integration.** Design a plan that includes all of the activities necessary to achieve objectives and integrate with business operations.

2.4.3 Implement Change

Planning, implementation, and transition processes are overlapping, as shown in Figure 2-5, which reinforces the concept that change implementation is an iterative process. Implementation more specifically concerns the process of successfully delivering project outputs to the business.

- **Prepare organization for change.** Identify areas where specific support is required and implement support activities.

- **Mobilize stakeholders.** Inform stakeholders of the ultimate objectives for the change and enable them to actively participate in decisions impacting the change.

- **Deliver project outputs.** Products, services, and results are considered to be outputs from the change initiative.

2.4.4 Manage Transition

The transition process links the change initiative with the operations side of the business and business as usual. It incorporates the measures to enable the organization to sustain long-term changes.

- **Transition outputs into business.** During the change process, as results are being delivered, continue the ongoing transition process by integrating the new capabilities into business as usual.

- **Measure adoption rate and outcomes/benefits.** Measure results at the business level, not just in terms of product results, but in terms of performance results.

- **Adjust plan to address discrepancies.** All change initiatives have a degree of uncertainty and ambiguity; therefore, the team needs to adjust the plan on a regular basis to account for changing or evolving circumstances.

2.4.5 Sustain Change

The success of any change initiative lies in the benefit value for the organization and its stakeholders; therefore it is important to sustain the change through a number of ongoing activities that exceed the traditional scope of projects and programs.

- **Ongoing communication, consultation, and representation of stakeholders.** Success of the change is reinforced by two-way communication and consultation with stakeholders.

- **Conduct sensemaking activities.** Ongoing conversation and social practices that enable people to make sense of what is happening during the change.

- **Measure benefits realization.** Measure success of the change through its impact on the organization.

2.5 Critical Factors that Can Impede or Foster Change

A substantial segment of the change management literature focuses on describing how managers and employees respond to change and advises managers and staff as to how to handle the stress, conflicts, and emotional issues that accompany change, gain support for and participation in the change effort, and generally make organization-wide changes less traumatic.

Change is implemented by and has consequences for people, and change can be made significantly less traumatic and more successful if these human aspects are anticipated and handled effectively. It is important to involve employees effectively in organizational decision making and change initiatives. During times of change, communication and stakeholder engagement are more important than usual and can substantially affect the cost and outcome of change efforts. Trust is identified as particularly important in obtaining support for and participation in change efforts. Executives and employees see change differently: (a) senior managers typically see change as an opportunity for both the business and themselves; and (b) employees typically see change as disruptive, intrusive, and likely to involve loss. When managing change, it is essential to identify the key issues, such as loss of turf, attachment, meaning, future, competency-based identity, and/or control.

2.6 Summary

Strategy execution occurs in a dynamic environment. The management of change within a dynamic environment, maintenance of strategy alignment, and cross-organizational integration with strategic changes are critical capabilities for successful execution and benefits realization. Portfolio, program, and project management translate strategy into action and are the catalysts through which strategy is achieved. Organizations also need to effectively and smoothly assimilate the impact of change resulting from the implementation of projects and programs. Both situations require good change management practice.

Change management is inherent in PMI's project and program management standards. It is embedded in the Process Groups and Knowledge Areas associated with stakeholder management, communications management, risk management, requirements management, governance, etc. In PMI's foundational standards, change management content is clearly more pronounced, particularly within the updated *PMBOK® Guide* – Fifth Edition, *The Standard for Program Management* – Third Edition, *The Standard for Portfolio Management* – Third Edition and *OPM3®*. Portfolio, program, and project management with well-executed change management are key business leadership skills required of portfolio, program, and project managers.

3

MANAGING CHANGE IN AN ORGANIZATIONAL PROJECT MANAGEMENT CONTEXT

3.1 Overview

This section describes change management in the context of organizational project management (OPM), which is a characteristic of high-performing organizations.

Key factors for successfully building a competitive advantage with the strategy execution framework of organizational project management are embedded with change management. These key factors address critical success factors, potential barriers, lack of synergy, and the capabilities of a sponsor function in the organization.

In today's continually evolving business environment, change is essential for organizations to stay competitive, and business strategies are frequently related to change. Strategy translates the vision and mission developed at the executive and portfolio levels into changes that will produce tangible benefits and deliver maximum value to stakeholders, ensuring continued growth and sustainable competitive advantage. These changes can be revolutionary such as a merger, acquisition, or business transformation, or evolutionary such as delivering new capabilities or services to the organization, for example, a new accounting system or an improved manufacturing process.

Project management, in terms of simply focusing on scope, time, and budget, is not sufficient for managing the scale and rate of change that is the norm in most organizations. Organizations that (a) drive portfolio, program, and project management strategically with top management visibility; (b) use active executive sponsors on programs and projects; and (c) use consistent and standardized practices are more successful at delivering projects on time and on budget. More importantly, these organizations meet their intended goals 80% of the time [9].

3.2 Description of OPM and Context

Organizations seek to improve their business outcomes and utilize many disciplines in order to improve their results. The project management discipline has been maturing for several decades as the approach of choice for many organizations to deliver change initiatives on time, on budget, and with the agreed-upon scope and quality.

Over the last decade, the disciplines of program and portfolio management gathered momentum as a means to manage initiatives. From a business perspective, program management focuses on the realization of the anticipated benefits of a group of synergistic work efforts. Portfolio management helps organizations to direct resources in order to move their strategy forward.

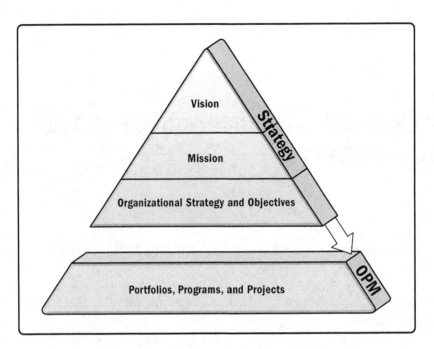

Figure 3-1. The Integrated Framework

When these disciplines are part of an integrated framework, as shown in Figure 3-1, organizations are able to deliver strategy in a successful manner. In order to deliver better organizational results, this framework needs to support and align the organization's components—people, process, structures, systems and technology—to effectively deliver business results with a focus on continuous improvement. This framework is called organizational project management (OPM).

3.2.1 Description of OPM

The *Organizational Project Management Maturity Model (OPM3®)* – Third Edition defines organizational project management as a strategy execution framework that utilizes portfolio, program, and project management as well as organizational-enabling practices to consistently and predictably deliver organizational strategy to produce better performance, better results, and a sustainable competitive advantage. Figure 3-2 (from *OPM3*) shows the OPM strategy execution framework and its component elements.

- **Strategy.** Organizational strategy is an input into the OPM strategy execution framework and is based on the organization's mission, vision, and values. This strategy is developed to deliver maximum value to the organization's stakeholders and create the desired business results for the organization. This strategy acts as the roadmap for the remaining elements of the OPM strategy execution framework.

- **Portfolio.** The organization uses portfolio management as a means to determine which initiatives the organization should undertake in order to fulfill its strategy. Portfolio management aligns the work and resources of the organization to deliver organizational strategy. The PMI foundational standard,

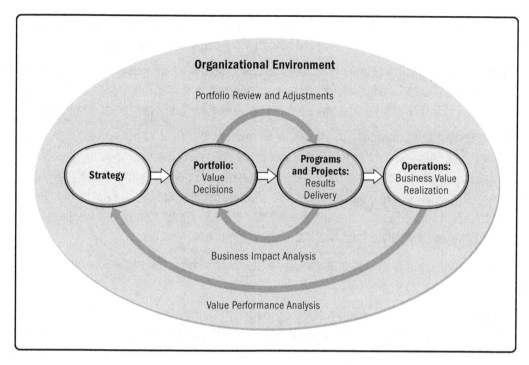

Figure 3-2. Organizational Project Management (Source: *OPM3®*, PMI: 2013)

The Standard for Portfolio Management – Third Edition, sets the groundwork for the portfolio processes in OPM. Section 4 of this practice guide discusses the relationship between portfolio management and change management.

- **Program and project management.** The organization uses program and project management as a means to effectively and efficiently deliver the initiatives of the organization. Strategy alignment continues through these disciplines and culminates with the realization of the value that each initiative has been commissioned to achieve. This achievement is apparent when the results of the initiative are transitioned to the operations of the organization. *A Guide to the Project Management Body of Knowledge (PMBOK® Guide)* – Fifth Edition and *The Standard for Program Management* – Third Edition are the basis for these processes in organizational project management. Sections 5 and 6 cover program and project management as they relate to change management.

- **Business impact analysis.** There are multiple analysis and feedback loops that are part of the OPM strategy execution framework. Business impact analysis collects results data from programs and projects and feeds it back into the portfolio. From these results, the impact on the business is then determined. A results assessment is completed at the end of programs and projects, but it is also performed at scheduled intervals (for programs) to produce insights that may lead to modifications of other portfolios.

- **Portfolio review and adjustments.** The intent of the portfolio review and adjustment loop is alignment and realignment to strategy. The portfolio analyzes current market trends, in addition to results from programs and projects, and adjusts the portfolio of initiatives to reflect these changing conditions.

- **Operations.** Outcomes of the programs and projects are transitioned into the operations area of the business where the business value of the completed initiatives is measured.

- **Value performance analysis.** This final feedback loop provides the business with value realization data delivered from programs and projects to business operations. It is an input for future strategy development as well as a measure of how well the intended benefits have achieved the strategic objectives.

- **Organizational environment.** An important element of the OPM strategy execution framework is the organizational environment itself. This represents the policies and supporting practices of the organization that are created to support the OPM strategy execution framework and delivery of the organization's strategy. These supporting practices are called organizational enablers (OE) and include the organizational competencies required to successfully deliver strategy. More importantly, this is where the integration of the OPM strategy execution framework and change management occur.

There are two fundamental premises that should be discussed in relation to OPM and the strategy execution framework:

- **Process improvement.** Creating a strategy execution framework is not a one-time activity. In order to fulfill the vision and mission of the organization, the OPM strategy execution framework needs to mature and evolve. Continuous process improvement should be part of the values of the organization and be applied to the framework in order for it to mature as the organization's strategy advances.

- **Context.** The context of an organization needs to be factored into its strategy. Context represents the environments in which an organization is situated and how it structures itself to respond to these environments. The primary environment is the industry in which the organization operates and competes. Other environments include the size and structure of the organization as well as its geographic distribution.

To summarize, OPM is a business approach for the deployment and delivery of organizational strategy through the harmonized and effective implementation of portfolio, program, and project management. It is important to mention that OPM is an adaptive approach for fitting the capabilities of portfolio, program, and project management to the unique context, circumstances, and needs of the organization. Process improvement principles may be applied to all of the disciplines of OPM to achieve the benefits of fit.

3.3 Change Management and OPM

Section 2 provided the background for change management and described change management as a comprehensive, cyclic, and structured approach for transitioning individuals, groups and organizations from a current state to a future state and intended business benefits. Change management helps organizations to integrate and align people, processes, structures, culture, and strategy. In the context of OPM, change management helps organizations successfully drive their strategy through the OPM elements of portfolio, program, and project management.

The *2012 Pulse of the Profession* study indicated that the failure rate for projects continues to increase. *Best Industry Outcomes* [7] research shows that fewer than 20% of organizations have change management capabilities.

Organizations that have some change management capabilities do not necessarily use those capabilities in an effective manner. The research identified a direct correlation between the underutilization of change management and the increase of project failure.

This research also provides data regarding the increasing size and scale of projects. Between 50% and 75% of the survey respondents noted that the size and scale of projects has a key correlation to project failure. The increase of uncertainty, volatility, and turbulence in the business environment increases the difficulty of delivering expected benefits of projects and programs.

Change management is one tool that organizations use for addressing a complex and high-risk business environment. Change management helps organizations to (a) adapt to more innovative thinking approaches, (b) expand their communications to ensure ongoing, shared vision, and (c) build rapid alignment to change.

Industries that reported using high levels of change management include:

- Aerospace/defense,
- Financial/business services,
- Fast moving consumer goods, and
- Government.

These industries face highly competitive markets, demanding customers, and complex political and social environments. In addition, these industries have naturally evolved to using change management to enable them to deal with ambiguity and volatility and still achieve the business outcomes they seek. Organizations seeking better business outcomes should consider how change management can help them to build the agility they need to respond to today's business challenges.

The use of portfolio, program, and project management with the feedback loops, described earlier in this section as the OPM strategy execution framework, are strengthened and sustained by the utilization of change management. Successful organizations are driving achievement of their strategic objectives with OPM and change management as shown in Figure 3-3.

3.3.1 Framing the Disciplines

Change management requires undertaking activities that align programs and projects with the strategy of the organization as well as activities that transition project results into operations to realize business benefits. Figure 3-4 shows the relationship between the change management life cycle framework and the rest of the OPM elements.

The OPM strategy execution framework integrates all of these disciplines to deliver change consistently and predictably to maintain or increase an organization's performance and sustain its competitive advantage.

Portfolio management is an ongoing management practice that consists of optimizing and overseeing a number of concurrent organizational initiatives. It entails the selection and authorization of activities based on defined

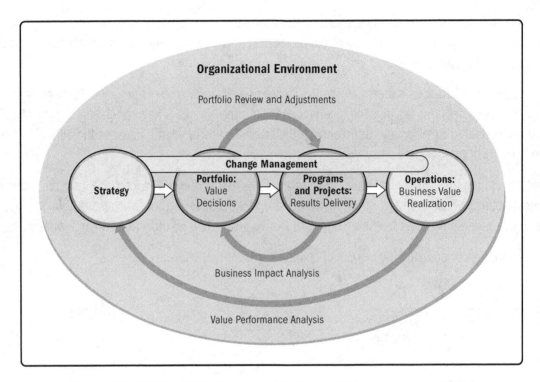

Figure 3-3. Driving Achievement with Change Management and OPM

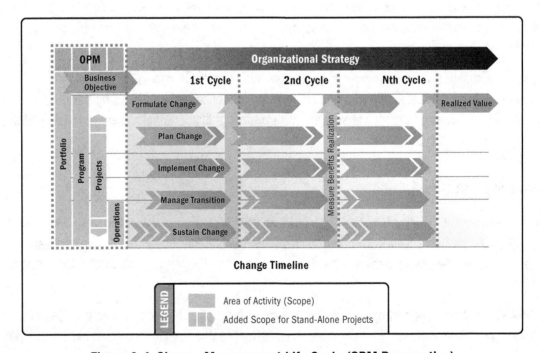

Figure 3-4. Change Management Life Cycle (OPM Perspective)

business objectives (including change formulation activities), dynamic evaluation of the initiatives' benefits, and adjustment or realignment of the portfolio of activities, if necessary, in addition to the management of its integration into the business to realize value and sustain competitive advantage.

Program management is a strategy implementation process that involves the definition of a set of expected benefits and the delivery and transition of those benefits into the business. A full program life cycle typically includes multiple iterations of the change life cycle phases in Figure 3-4. Program components, including projects, are integrated under the program umbrella to facilitate the management and delivery of benefits in a paced sequence. Typically, a full project life cycle, from initiation to closure, is included in one program cycle; however, some projects may extend over more than one cycle.

Programs have a significant element of associated ambiguity and uncertainty, which prevents the full suite of program activities from being known at the time of the program definition phase. In contrast, projects require well-defined beginnings and boundaries, including a statement of work that describes the products, services, or results that the project will deliver and the relationship of the project deliverables to the business need that the project addresses.

The scope of a stand-alone project may extend beyond the typical boundaries of a project to include (a) initiation activities before the project is formally chartered and (b) transition activities in order to deliver and sustain the change successfully. These activities may include change formulation and planning activities as well as ongoing activities, such as product support and service management. They may also include change management, user engagement, or customer support activities that may extend beyond the traditional project scope.

The change process spans all levels of a business; it typically stems from strategic objectives that are part of an overall organizational strategy and are set at the portfolio level. Programs and stand-alone projects begin with the formulation of the change and its planning; change is then implemented through one or more projects that produce tangible deliverables (products, services, and results) for the business. These deliverables are transitioned into the business as usual (operations) to produce benefits and, when it is sustained over time, value for the organization and its stakeholders. Figure 3-4 also shows change as a cyclic process that needs to be planned, based on the organization's capabilities, structures, and culture.

3.3.2 Cycles of Change

Figure 3-5 shows the level of effort required in each OPM domain during a complete change life cycle process; it is worthwhile noting the difference in the level of effort between each of the OPM disciplines, because it will enable managers to understand the need to involve different stakeholders at different times during the full change life cycle. Note that while portfolio management activities are ongoing, the activities can cover multiple changes at the same time. However, for a single change process, the effort is greatest (a) during change formulation when the organizational initiatives are selected and approved, and (b) during benefits measurement when the organizational impact of the change is assessed. This helps guide portfolio decisions concerning the next cycle. Throughout the remainder of the change cycle, portfolio activities consist essentially of monitoring activities.

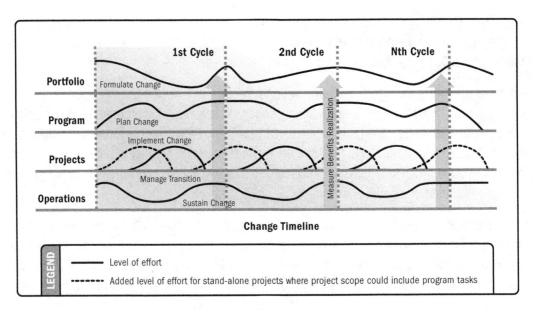

Figure 3-5. Change Life Cycles

In the case of program management, activities are at a high level throughout the entire change life cycle with dips during implementation where activities mostly cover component (project) oversight and integration. At the end of the full cycle when the program ends, activities fall to zero.

In the case of projects, the level of effort follows a typical "S" curve pattern from initiation (change planning) to closure (change transition). As stated previously, stand-alone projects may incorporate a continuous activity level to formulate the change and transition it into business as usual.

Operations typically include both the initiators and beneficiaries of the change, and their involvement will be greatest at formulation when they need to identify and clarify the need for change and participate in the change planning. These functions will be engaged on a continuous basis throughout the change, but their active participation will be requested during transition activities when they will be required to integrate the change into their business-as-usual activities.

3.4 Assessing Change Readiness

The description of change management in the OPM context is not complete until the subject of change readiness and the change readiness assessment is explored. Change readiness refers to an optimal state of acceptance demonstrated by an organization. The change readiness assessment measures the reality of the current organization in relation to the future state.

Change readiness is assessed from two perspectives:

- Organizational systems and structures that need to be improved or will support the change, and

- People and culture that are able to support or may resist the change.

From both perspectives, the context should include an assessment of the impact of the change initiatives that are undertaken by, or impacting on, the organization and the organization's capability and capacity to absorb change. Even organizations that have a high capacity for change will have a tipping point, and exceeding this tipping point could jeopardize the organization's ability to deliver its strategic objectives.

Change readiness can be accomplished at single or multiple levels of the organization or across the entire organization. Organizational systems are considered in their entirety and should not be considered independently from one another. Generally, there are many interdependencies between systems, and these should be identified and integrated with the change plan. Change readiness performed at an organizational level provides insights to the interdependencies of the entire system.

When determining an organization's preparedness for change, the following elements should be considered as part of the assessment:

- **Culture and historical experience in dealing with change.** It answers the question "What systemic attitudes, aids, and impediments exist in the organization that are likely to impact the process of achieving change?"

- **Policies, processes, roles, and decision-making norms related to change management.** It answers the question "How well does the organization function in a well-defined manner during change efforts?"

- **Accountability hierarchy.** Sometimes called performance management, accountability hierarchy refers to the processes by which the organization holds people accountable. Implementation of change, by definition, affects the work for which people are held accountable. It answers the question "Can the organization hold its employees accountable?"

- **Change agenda: size, timeframe, and concurrency.** It answers the question "How well positioned is the organization to be able to absorb all the changes planned without creating significant risk of overload in affected areas?"

- **Resources applied to change management and their degree of expertise and experience.** It answers the question "What capability and experience base is available in the organization to assure well-coordinated change management activities around communication, process design, organizational structure design, and human resources planning?"

- **Leadership's capability of supporting and sponsoring change.** It answers the question "What leadership capability does the organization have and how well will change be supported to achieve organizational goals?"

Change readiness is measured at the portfolio, program, and project levels; in each case, the level and range of measurements will be different. Change readiness can be measured by project and program managers, but is most effective when addressed by a portfolio manager. Readiness assessments should be a standard practice for each of these domains. These assessments provide insights for the broad view of the portfolio, the benefit realization view of programs, and the specific objectives of a single project. Each type of readiness assessment provides value at every level. When dealing with a specific change effort, the following elements should be considered part of the assessment.

- **Motivations, barriers, and limitations to moving forward on a particular change effort.** It answers the question "What drives/creates desire for the envisioned change, and what creates impediments or speed bumps?"

- **Context for the change.** This includes such factors as marketplace conditions, competition, windows of opportunity, other changes competing for organizational resources, and the political environment. It answers the question, "In what set of contexts does the change need to be successful?"

- **People and organizations.** This addresses those that need to be involved in the change and the degree to which they are knowledgeable about the proposed change. It answers the question, "Have we accurately identified all stakeholders and their vested interests, and are they aware of the potential change and its intended benefits?"

- **Support and resources associated with a particular change effort.** It answers the question "What is needed to reduce impediments and enhance support for the envisioned change?"

Change readiness assessments are administered in any manner that an organization sees fit. Organizations commonly use surveys, interviews, or meetings and focus groups. In any case, however, change readiness is collated at the organizational level because all of the change elements, at every level, can have an influence on each other.

3.5 Key Factors for Change Management in the Execution of Organizational Project Management

This section provides an organization leader with factors that should be considered when achieving strategic results through the OPM strategy execution framework with change management. Success factors in addition to factors that can undermine an organization's success are explored.

3.5.1 Critical Success Factors

Key success factors underlie the practice of change management in organizational project management. While the methods used may vary, success is predicated on carefully addressing these principles.

3.5.1.1 Stakeholder Collaboration, Empowerment, and Engagement

- **Address stakeholders systematically and iteratively.** People tend to view human emotions and reactions as being unpredictable or even uncontrollable forces. However, much of human nature is predictable and, therefore, reacts predictably to certain interventions. Understanding how human nature works, planning for likely issues, and monitoring and correcting for changes are the most important aspects of change management in project management. In addition, it is important that project managers repeat iterations of obtaining input from those affected and repeat iterations of skill building and development.

- **Perform change "with" rather than "to" people.** Much of early change management theory offered the top-down perspective of leaders telling people about the change and then empowering them to implement change. Nothing creates a greater barrier to change than people who feel that they did not have input into a change. Buy-in does not occur when a business solution is carefully researched and rationally selected. When stakeholders are not part of the research and selection, they may be resistant to the solution.

Top-down scope definition often fails to account for potential barriers to acceptance and use of the deliverables of the project, or potential opportunities to maximize the benefit with little additional cost. The most crucial success factors in change management are: (a) ensuring those impacted by the change see the need for change, (b) determining the degree and nature of change that stakeholders believe is necessary to solve a problem or benefit from an opportunity, and (c) determining the scope and implementation plan options to effectively address the need or opportunity with the least amount of disruption. Ensuring that project plans incorporate these involvement activities is a crucial factor in change management success and helps the project manager avoid barriers to acceptance.

3.5.1.2 Allocate Time for Acceptance into the Change Life Cycle Framework

- **Build in flexibility.** Successful planning takes into consideration the human impact. In some cases, expected resistance may not materialize; in other cases, a seemingly innocuous change may create a viral reaction. Allocating time into the project/program schedule at key stages, while seemingly arbitrary, will ensure that the iterative activities of change management to address foreseen or emergent resistance will not impact the project schedule.

3.5.1.3 Ensure System Alignment with the Change Initiative

- **Ensure all supporting systems work effectively and efficiently together.** Change is multidimensional. Changing a software system, for example, usually requires changing work processes and may require new or different skillsets, work associates, roles and responsibilities, work environments, and possibly alter long-standing cultural norms. A strong change management plan ensures that all of these systems are change ready and able to interact effectively together.

- **Scale change management activities to the extent, complexity, and speed of the change.** Change management activities are scalable. Change management intensity is directly proportional to the number of people, systems, and processes that are affected and the sensitivity of the individual or group (for example, job status, compensation, individual or team purpose/value/importance to the organization). Negative emotional reaction is also proportional to the speed of the change, so if a change needs to happen quickly, more intense change management activity is warranted.

3.5.1.4 Provide Focus for the Change Initiative

- **Create a clear description and measures for a successful future state.** When benefits realized are the measures of change management success, a clear definition of the future state is crucial in assessing how well the project has contributed to that new state. Quantitative and qualitative measures of benefits realized are difficult to establish when the picture of the future state is not detailed or descriptive. Program and project managers need to elicit the specific requirements of the deliverables in addition to the intended use and value of those deliverables so that the delivered output fulfills its intent.

- **Provide strong sponsorship for change initiatives.** Best-in-class OPM organizations establish strong sponsorship for projects. The sponsor provides leadership, resources, and support of the change initiative and helps to establish the compelling opportunity and vision for the initiative. The sponsor acts as the spokesperson on behalf of the initiative, promoting the merits of the change to all levels of management. Additionally, the sponsor works with superiors, peers, and subordinates to assist the project/program manager effect the change.

- **Build communication assets.** Communication is a key factor in change management. Organizations build reusable communication assets that can be used by the lead function. These assets include communication models, communication methods, and communication requirements methods. These communications assets are critical as projects and programs become larger in scale and more complex, and team members are geographically distributed.

One of the most challenging and demanding aspects of any change initiative is communication. Communication is the key to engaging people in the change. Successful change relies heavily on how the participants view it. When any kind of change is announced, people want information. When communications are insufficient, change can be delayed because people will continue to work as they have in the past rather than risk performing incorrectly. Effective communication is designed to create awareness and understanding in order to get subsequent supportive action. The rationale is that people are more likely to buy-in to change if they understand the benefits of the change. Successful change requires the majority of stakeholders to accept the change and commit to the direction that the organization is establishing.

Effective communication requires a deliberate plan for determining who needs to understand the what, why, when, and how of the change. The best time to map out what communications are required is during the early planning stage for the change. Good communication should never be an afterthought, but rather a significant part of the portfolio, program, or project plan. It should reflect the specific needs and complexity of the change and may be formal or informal, highly detailed, or broadly structured. As with all other planning documents prepared at the start of a change, the communication plan should be a living document that is subject to regular review and credible in its content to ensure the change intent is maintained.

- **Clearly communicate the change vision early.** Establish the foundation for the change by clearly communicating the vision for the organization at the end of the change. The vision should be clear, compelling, described in simple terms, and capable of being used as a guide for change decisions and outcomes. It will be easier for people to adapt to the change if it is communicated early in the change process.

- **Outline the benefits and impacts of the change.** Communicate to overcome the fears and concerns aroused by change, explain why the change is happening, and what the change will mean in the long run. People want to know how change will affect them. (Will they still have a job after the change? Will they maintain their position? Will they have an interesting role? What will their future be?) Uncertainty in a working environment reduces productivity; therefore, it is important to communicate what is changing and why. Stakeholders need to know who will be affected and how, why it is happening, and what the timelines are for the change.

- **Ensure that the organization's leaders actively communicate throughout the change process.** It is important that the organization's leaders publicly show commitment to the change. The personal and visible involvement of the organization's leaders in communicating the change sends a powerful message to stakeholders about how serious the organization is in implementing the change. This is not something that should be delegated. Active and visible management commitment gives credibility to communications, demonstrates management's ownership to doing business in a different way, and encourages a greater degree of stakeholder acceptance.

- **Use multiple methods and channels to communicate.** Some people are visual learners and are best approached with written material. Others do better by listening and responding to the spoken word. Analysis should be done to determine the best form of communication channel for the message. Communicating face-to-face is believed to be the richest form of communication and may be warranted on most change efforts.

- **Provide opportunities for dialogue and true representation.** The more dramatic the change is—the greater the need for two-way communication and active stakeholder participation. Provide opportunities to mobilize and engage stakeholders so as to promote a sense of ownership and to inform stakeholders that their opinions are important and their comments and suggestions are valued.

- **Repeat the change messages often.** Once the case for change is communicated and it is clear that change is going to happen, regular communication is a priority. Provide opportunities for people to hear and question information. People who have worked on a project for a long period of time may become so entrenched in the work that they forget the change message. People who leave projects and return at a later phase must be reminded of the change message. Repetition of clear and compelling change messages using multiple channels greatly increases the probability that the information will be understood. Repeated messages, but with small tweaks, may be needed to fine tune the change message.

- **Monitor and measure the effectiveness of the communications.** Although time-intensive, the effort of monitoring and measuring results is vital for gauging key stakeholders' reactions to communications. It is rare that people hear exactly what is intended in a message the first time, and monitoring provides an opportunity to determine the stakeholders' level of awareness and attitudes, address instances of misinformation, identify and address ongoing issues, and adjust or tailor the information to suit the needs of the change participants.

3.5.1.5 Identify, Select, and Develop Talent Based on Change Management Competencies

- **Change management competency program.** Organizations that embrace talent management establish competency development programs for project managers and team members. Organizations that adopt change management as a key capability build competency development programs for the knowledge, skills, and proficiencies needed to effectively execute change.

- **Build a change management training curriculum.** Organizations establish change management training programs for all roles of the organization—project team members, executives, middle managers, and supervisors. This approach utilizes educational programs to build knowledge about change management in the organization. Part of the change management curriculum needs to address the skills required for change management, for example, exploiting and embracing change.

- **Capture and share lessons learned.** Organizations that have successful change programs capture the lessons learned from each of those initiatives. These lessons learned are retained in a knowledge management repository. Prior to initiating a new change, the organization requires a review of the previous lessons learned.

- **Develop employees.** Employee involvement is important for successful change management. While change is managed at the organizational level, it addresses how to facilitate change at the individual level. Change research shows that employee involvement (helping people feel that they are in control of the change in their lives) facilitates the process.

3.5.1.6 Formalize Philosophy and Policy of Change Management

- **Establish change management policies.** Establish a culture for change management by writing policies or incorporating change statements into the vision and mission of the organization. Once policies are in place, require change management plans for all new initiatives. This approach requires change management to be applied for every major change initiative in the organization prior to receiving business case approval. Some organizations build an investment threshold by requiring change management processes for any project over a specified dollar amount.

- **Build a common change vocabulary.** Establish a standardized change methodology as the first step in establishing a common change vocabulary. Organizations need to spend sufficient time to drive the use of common terminology in order to guarantee awareness and adoption of the changes they are supporting.

3.5.1.7 Develop and Deploy Change Management Measurement Processes and Tools

- **Measure the success and sustainment of change.** Measurement is the instrument panel for change. Determine what existing organizational indicators are in place for measuring change. When existing systems are not in place, establish the measurement systems as the first part of any change initiative. This provides organizations with the indicators to allow course corrections for delivering the right benefits.

3.5.2 Potential Barriers and Change Derailers

It is likely that change will be met with resistance and potentially be derailed throughout all phases or steps in the change initiative. It is not uncommon for large, multimillion-dollar systems implementation projects to derail due to poor management of change. Change resistance should be measured for all stakeholders as changes are announced along with ongoing sampling at key points to monitor potential resistance throughout the change initiative. Sample items that are typically included in a change resistance survey include:

- Do you believe that this change is really needed?
- How involved have you been in the planning for this change?
- How clear has communication been about this change?
- How has the sponsor enabled the change to overcome organizational barriers?
- Do you believe that adequate rewards are being provided to accomplish this change?
- How compatible do you believe this change is with existing organizational values?
- How does this change align, support, or change other organization processes?

- To what degree have you been engaged in the change management steps, tools, and processes throughout the entire life cycle of the change?

- Do you believe that your supervisor or other members of the leadership team are genuinely supportive of this change?

Determine an overall resistance score including a resistance score for each of the stakeholder groups. If resistance is overt, the sponsor and those fulfilling the lead function can address this through effective problem-solving meetings. However, if it is covert, the sponsor and lead(s) will need to work openly with stakeholders to allow the issues to surface.

Some of the typical barriers to change that can derail change initiatives are provided in 3.5.2.1 through 3.5.2.7.

3.5.2.1 Lack of Good Sponsorship

- **Lack of a sponsor.** The sponsor function ensures organizational commitment to the change process and deals with issues encountered when implementing the desired action. In general, the higher the sponsor is in the organizational hierarchy, the greater chance of success in fully deploying the change. An organization's business strategy often exists as the vision of its CEO. In an evolving organization, documenting the vision of the future structure of the organization is required to articulate the strategy in enough detail to make sense to all employees. In many organizations, the ability to carry the vision throughout the organization is complicated by poor planning. For example, when organizations downsize by removing one or two layers of management, a substitute communications model needs to be created to reestablish clear channels of communication and interfaces of roles and responsibilities.

- **Lack of commitment to funding and/or resources.** Change requires the commitment of time and resources by the organization. Employees and leaders need time to consider the impacts of the change as well as the required methods, tools, and skills. This may create a lag between the implementation of the changes and realization of the benefits. Organizations that do not address this issue effectively often do not provide sufficient commitment to the change efforts. This lack of commitment is often due to shortage of funding dollars, shortage of time to plan effectively and implement the change efforts, or insufficient resources (e.g., people, tools, equipment, and systems) to implement the change successfully.

3.5.2.2 Cultural Resistance to Change

- **Culture that resists change.** Corporate culture is the greatest barrier to successful implementation of change. There are a variety of issues for organizations to overcome:

  - *Inertia.* Frequently the leadership sees the need for change, but is hampered by a workforce threatened by the perceived sacrifices. Conversely, corporate leaders who insulate themselves from day-to-day interaction with customers, operations personnel, and first-line management are the last to recognize that change is needed.

  - *Trust.* A lack of trust inhibits members of an organization from devising and executing a plan for change. Management needs to believe in the basic competence of the organization's personnel to learn how much the team can be challenged and how much they can achieve.

○ *Competencies.* Many organizations lack the competencies to change. A workforce that has no exposure to world-class business models and change methods can hardly be expected to adapt to a new structure. Training key managers is not enough. Basic education and advanced knowledge of adaptive systems throughout the organization is key to successful change management. The entire workforce needs to understand the change model that the organization is going to use. If everyone understands the path for change, the workforce can move in the same direction.

○ *Bureaucracy.* Bureaucratic corporate decision processes often do not support growth and adaptation. As corporate structures evolve, there is a natural tendency for decisions to be made at the highest level. This creates a decision process that is cumbersome and divorced from accurate and current information. The decision support structure should allow for long-term strategic decisions to be made at the corporate level, tactical decisions to be made at the point of engagement, and operational decisions to be made by front-line employees.

3.5.2.3 Failure to Build Change Readiness

- **Lack of recognition for the need to continuously change.** Managers sometimes do not recognize the need to make changes in their businesses. This may be due to current success and not understanding that today's methods are becoming less relevant to tomorrow's success. Additionally, it may be caused by failure to recognize new competitors from areas outside of their immediate market segment. Management's way of viewing its world creates a framework for determining the type of information it considers to be important. Information outside of this framework is generally considered of little importance or is ignored completely. These circumstances cause the organization to appear not to recognize the need to change.

- **Lack of knowledge/learning in a change process.** When employees do not understand how to implement change or several different methods are applied for the same change initiative, the organization will not succeed in implementing the desired change. This is common in organizations that do not train all employees in change methodology or create an environment where the methodology is used.

3.5.2.4 Insufficient Time Allocated to Change

- **Lack of time.** When insufficient time for implementation is allotted, huge post-change maintenance costs will result. Organizations should allot time for the recipients to internalize or adapt to the principles of the change.

- **Poor follow through.** Many organizations launch major projects with great fanfare and reward those responsible for initiating the change, but then fail to follow through to see that the initiative achieved its stated goals.

3.5.2.5 Poor Vision of the Future

- **Lack of a clear vision of the future.** Change requires many people to perform their daily routine work in a different manner. These actions are rarely specified in procedures or detailed manuals. If a consistent, clear picture of the future state toward which the organization is driving does not exist in each individual's mind, their daily decisions will not help move the organization toward the vision.

3.5.2.6 Poor Access to Technology by All Stakeholders

- **Lack of access to technology.** Technology is rarely a barrier to the successful implementation of change in an organization. Typically technology is available, but not effectively used; large expenditures are made, but results fall short of expectations. The decision to overlay a business process with a particular technology is difficult to make, and costly mistakes occur frequently. Intranets, extranets, the Internet, and wideband video capability are excellent tools for rapid knowledge dissemination. Buying-in to an emerging technology too early leads to higher acquisition costs and higher risk due to the potential for changes in standards or quick obsolescence if the technology is not widely accepted. Conversely, waiting too long to abandon an aging technology subjects organizations to expenses associated with maintaining systems and products after the larger marketplace has passed them by.

  There are few decision models for determining when to transition to a downstream technology. Trying to maintain a corporation's current technological framework when technological products and processes are fluid is difficult. In addition, there are few reliable models that lead to any understanding of return on an investment in information technology. The ability for personnel to absorb a new technology is often less than adequate, both in terms of new skill sets that are required and in terms of attitude or willingness to embrace the new technology. New technology usually requires significant changes to processes and practices, and organization managers may be unwilling to pay for specific training. This forces employees to learn "on the fly" and at their own expense, which affects morale and prevents the organization from realizing the benefits of the technology.

3.5.2.7 Poor Measures and/or Measurement Process

- **Lack of performance metrics.** Change initiatives requiring significant expenditures need to focus on high-leverage issues. Successful change requires organizations to effectively measure results before, during, and after the change. When these metrics are not defined, change initiatives may drift, fail, or be perceived as successful when in fact they are not. Additionally, change initiatives focused in low-leverage areas should have future high potential to warrant their support. These decisions can only be made with facts and metrics; otherwise emotional and political barriers may derail the change efforts.

3.5.3 Lack of Synergy within the Affected Group and Dominant Individuals

When attempting to make a change, it is important to examine the relationships among the key sponsors, recipients, and agents. These relationships may be viewed as self-destructive, static, or synergistic. Self-destructive relationships require significant energy to sustain, but produce few, if any, results. Such relationships usually are full of miscommunication, defensiveness, and blaming. Static relationships have an even mix of negative, backstabbing behavior, and productive, team-oriented behavior. People in this situation are as effective working together as they are working alone. Synergistic relationships create a sum that is greater than its parts. Each individual willingly contributes a part of their expertise that is needed by the others; as a result, change is brought about quickly, and the team's productivity soars above what each individual could have done alone.

Mobilizing stakeholders is an obvious issue in any program, but difficult to accomplish. One of the best methods to mobilize stakeholders is to empower them through distributed control; however, this requires a cultural approach that organization leadership may be reluctant to consider. This approach could also have issues for coordination to ensure that no gaps exist. In order to empower employees and team members, they need to become aware of the ultimate objectives and purpose of the change. Then the organization can empower them to make decisions within their function's responsibility and allow them to actively participate in higher-level decision processes creating true "transforming" exchanges that influence outcomes.

Designing meaningful stakeholder involvement in the change initiative is a significant task, and stakeholder analysis is typically performed in the communications management plan for the change. The larger and more disruptive the change, the more vital it becomes to assess different participants' influence on the change.

People resist change for a number of reasons: self-interest, denial, fear of the unknown, or other perceptions. When the root of possible resistance to change is understood, then planning for it makes it possible to overcome potential obstacles. Stakeholder analysis is an important means of uncovering potential pockets of resistance or other risks that could impede the success of the change. Regardless of the size of the change, stakeholder analysis is a useful way to:

- Determine specific stakeholders or stakeholder groups and their relationships to the change,
- Identify current attitudes toward the change and level of influence,
- Identify communication needs and any risks associated with not meeting these needs, and
- Determine the mechanisms and timing for delivering change messages to meet the needs.

The project or program team is better able to define the appropriate communication for each audience when there is understanding of the attitudes and feelings toward the change effort. Without a stakeholder analysis and evaluation of the risk involved, the change team risks communicating inappropriately, resulting in stakeholder conflicts and uncertainty. Without understanding stakeholder motivations, needs, and expectations, it is difficult to overcome obstacles, and stakeholders may continue to be confrontational and cause conflicts throughout the change process.

3.5.4 Capabilities of Sponsors

Today's new business environment requires agile leaders who possess the capability to sense and respond to changes with actions that are focused, fast, and flexible. One tool that organizations can use to select and develop qualified sponsors is the leadership 360-degree assessment, which measures the following major capabilities of sponsorship:

- Anticipates change,
- Generates confidence,
- Initiates action,
- Liberates thinking, and
- Evaluates results.

Successful change management requires a large commitment from an organization's leaders, regardless of whether the change is occurring in a single section or across the entire organization. Change is inherently unsettling for people, and when it occurs, all eyes turn to the organization's leaders for support and direction. Leaders play a key role by promoting and sustaining the impetus for the change, coaching employees and executives, and communicating a shared sense of the path forward.

Fundamentally, the onus is on the organization's leaders to change first, motivate the rest of the organization, and set the example by displaying the desired behavior. Support and commitment from all leaders (both formal and informal) is critical for the acceptance of change within an organization. Leaders should delegate responsibility and empower others to make decisions about the change that is grounded with a clear change vision. Delegation of decision-making authority helps to reduce blockages and increases buy-in from people affected by the change. Leaders and managers throughout the organization should be expected to support and communicate the benefits of change to their peers and employees. Change needs to cascade through the organization because change occurs at each level. In order to accomplish this, leaders need to assume ownership for the change and be willing to accept responsibility for making it happen in all areas that they influence or manage.

A key responsibility of the sponsor function is to ensure that the organization's leaders continue to be involved throughout the entire change life cycle. Sponsor involvement needs to be evident in each phase, from initiation and planning through implementation. Leaders need to continuously engage with stakeholders. Key responsibilities for an organization's leaders throughout the change process are to:

- **Assess readiness and make adjustments.** The state of readiness for change shifts over time, and may differ in various parts of the organization. Change is dynamic and will require adjustment/correction to achieve desired outcomes. Organizational leaders play an important role in monitoring, assessing, and understanding each area's capacity to take on and succeed in change. Leaders should be able to form a highly accurate picture of the way the organization is progressing with the change and to determine what specifically needs to be done to enhance the likelihood of change success. When assessing change readiness across the organization, potential roadblocks, areas requiring remedial action, and areas of best practice can be identified.

- **Take action and resolve issues.** Throughout the change process, issues may arise that require the organization's leaders to intervene and take decisive action. Leaders should have the authority to make decisions regarding issues that impact the organization; escalate issues to more senior leadership, when applicable; and push for timely resolution or delegate that authority to others and support the final decision.

3.6 Summary

Successful change management provides organizations with a competitive advantage. High-performing organizations accomplish strategic change by using portfolio, program and project management. A few critical success factors for successful change management are: effective communication, addressing potential resistance, team collaboration, and the active support of the sponsor.

The use of portfolio, program, and project management in an organization is also strengthened by recognizing the elements of change management inherent in them. The subsequent sections in this practice guide expand on this foundation and address the specific change management characteristics in the portfolio, program, and project domains.

CHANGE MANAGEMENT AT THE PORTFOLIO LEVEL

4

4.1 Overview

Executing strategy well requires the successful delivery of change programs—programs to improve performance and implement innovations. This section examines change management as a function of managing portfolios of programs and projects—an important and complex task involving many different roles and functions, and prompting strong emotional feelings of attachment to particular initiatives on the part of senior managers and other major stakeholders.

The ten underlying principles and practices of portfolio management contained in the *Standard for Portfolio Management* – Third Edition are described, and the explicit considerations involved in change management are developed for each of the three Portfolio Management Process Groups: Defining, Aligning, and Authorizing and Controlling Process Groups.

A checklist is provided for conducting a change impact gap analysis to determine the extent to which an organization is positioned to absorb the changes implicit in a specific initiative.

4.2 The Standard for Portfolio Management

The Standard for Portfolio Management – Third Edition identifies portfolio management processes generally recognized as good practices. "Generally recognized" means that the knowledge and practices described are appropriate to most portfolios most of the time, and that there is widespread consensus about their value and usefulness. "Good practice" means there is general agreement that the application of these skills, tools, and techniques can enhance the chances of success over a wide range of portfolios. Good practice does not mean the knowledge described should always be applied uniformly to all portfolios; the organization and portfolio manager are responsible for determining what is appropriate for any given portfolio.

4.2.1 What Is a Portfolio?

A portfolio has the following characteristics:

- A portfolio is a component collection of programs, projects, or operations managed as a group to achieve strategic objectives.
- The portfolio components may not necessarily be interdependent or have related objectives.
- The portfolio components are quantifiable, that is, they may be measured, ranked, and prioritized.
- A portfolio exists to achieve one or more organizational strategies and objectives and may consist of a set of past, current, and planned or future portfolio components.

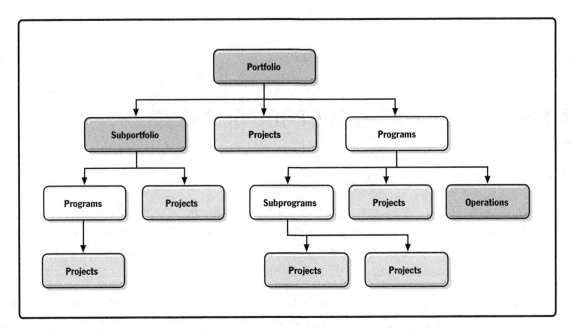

Figure 4-1. Portfolios, Programs, and Projects – High-Level View

- An organization may have more than one portfolio, each addressing unique organizational strategies and objectives.

- Proposed initiatives are structured as portfolios and components are identified, evaluated, selected, and authorized.

Practitioners working at the portfolio management level should be thoroughly familiar with the content of *The Standard for Portfolio Management* – Third Edition. A high-level view of portfolios as related to programs and projects is shown in Figure 4-1. Note that portfolios may contain subportfolios.

4.2.2 Strategy Execution and Change Management

Portfolio management is an ongoing practice of optimizing and overseeing a number of concurrent organizational initiatives. It entails the selection and authorization of initiatives requiring change based on defined business objectives (including change formulation activities). Portfolio management facilitates the dynamic evaluation of these initiatives and adjustment or realignment of the portfolio activities, when necessary, including the management of their integration into the business to realize benefit value and sustain competitive advantage.

Managing change requires a clear vision of the future state. Strategic initiatives comprised of programs and projects move the organization towards that future state. Initiatives frequently involve a combination of one or more of the following:

- New products,
- New business models,
- New capabilities,
- New markets,

- New channels,

- New value creation opportunities, and

- Breakthrough platforms.

Change management is a significant factor in these value-creation opportunities. It is essential that all relevant stakeholders be involved in the development and execution of the individual components of the portfolio of programs and projects that seek to fulfill the strategic initiatives. Involving stakeholders as early as possible facilitates buy-in, generally improves the robustness of the component programs and projects, and increases the potential for successful benefits realization from the change.

Figure 4-2 depicts a portfolio and its component parts (programs and projects) for five business areas designed to reach the future state. This figure provides an example of a method for performing portfolio analysis whereby the dependencies and potential conflicts are identified. The portfolio roadmap uses this information to provide high-level strategic direction and information in a chronological fashion for portfolio management execution and

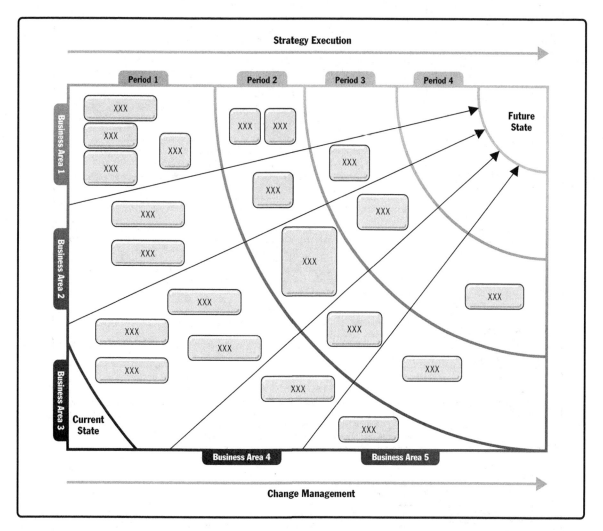

Figure 4-2. Strategy Execution and Change Management Moving towards the Future State

ensures that dependencies within the portfolio are established and evaluated. This is an essential component in enabling the management of the portfolio and demonstrating a clear path from the current state to the future state. Reviewing and updating the portfolio roadmap ensures alignment when changes occur and serves as a means for evaluating potential change saturation as outputs are delivered. Figure 4-2 also illustrates strategy execution and change management impact as the portfolio moves towards the future state.

4.2.3 Ten Underlying Principles and Practices of Portfolio Management

The ten underlying principles and practices of portfolio management contained in *The Standard for Portfolio Management* – Third Edition are described in Table 4-1.

Table 4-1. Ten Underlying Principles and Practices of Portfolio Management

1. Strategic Focus	Portfolio management is the coordinated management of one or more portfolios to achieve the strategies and objectives of the organization.
	It includes related organizational processes and change initiatives by which an organization evaluates, selects, prioritizes, and allocates its limited internal resources to best accomplish organizational strategies consistent with its vision, mission, and values.
2. Strategic Initiatives	Organizations execute their strategies through the creation of strategic initiatives, comprising portfolios of programs and projects to achieve a future state. The portfolio components may not necessarily be interdependent or have related objectives.
	An organization may have more than one portfolio, each addressing unique organizational strategies and objectives. Proposed initiatives are structured as portfolios and components are identified, evaluated, selected, and authorized. Managing the necessary changes should be an integral part of planning initiatives.
3. Portfolio Components	As shown in Figure 4-1, a portfolio is a component collection of related programs, projects, or operations managed as a group to achieve strategic objectives.
	A portfolio exists to achieve one or more organizational strategies and objectives and may consist of a set of past, current, and planned or future portfolio components.
4. Quantifiable Components	The portfolio components are quantifiable, that is, they can be measured, ranked, and prioritized.
5. Time Horizon	Portfolios and programs have the potential to be longer term with new projects rotating into the portfolios unlike projects, which have a defined beginning and end.
6. Portfolio Snapshot	At any given moment, a portfolio represents a snapshot of its selected portfolio components and reflects the organizational strategy and objectives—even when specific programs or projects within the portfolio are not interdependent or do not have related objectives.
7. Portfolio Management Activities	By reflecting upon the investments made or planned by an organization, portfolio management includes activities for identifying and aligning the organizational priorities; determining governance and performance management framework; measuring value/benefit; making investment decisions; and managing risk, communications, and resources.
8. Alignment to Organization Strategy	When elements of the portfolio are not aligned to organizational strategy, the organization should question why the work is being undertaken.
	A portfolio should be representative of an organization's intent, direction, and progress. It is possible to undertake essential projects that do not strictly align with the strategic portfolio. However, when these projects cannot be justified as essential, the portfolio manager should remove them from the portfolio of activities for reconsideration at a later date.
9. Governance	Portfolio management requires a governing body to make decisions that control or influence the direction of a group of portfolio components as they work to achieve specific outcomes.
	This governing body needs to be particularly sensitive to the degree of change required to achieve the portfolio initiatives.
10. Balancing of Conflicting Demands	Portfolio management balances conflicting demands between programs and projects, allocates resources (e.g., people and funding) based on organizational priorities and capacity, and manages resources in order to achieve the benefits identified.

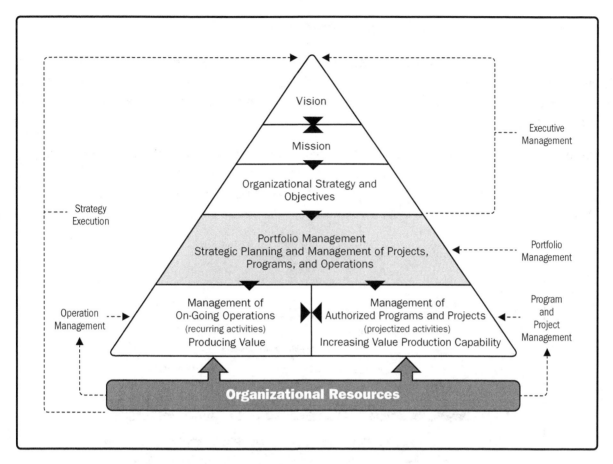

Figure 4-3. Organizational Context of Portfolio Management

The organizational context of strategy execution is shown in Figure 4-3. Portfolio management and the portfolio manager are located in the organization layer between the decision-making executive management team, and the project and program management organizations and operations management (OM).

Top to bottom strategy execution is variable between organizations. This practice guide is designed to improve the ability of organizations to successfully manage change. Toward that objective, a change impact assessment has been developed to facilitate managing change in organizations at the portfolio level and is described in Section 4.3.3.1.

While not all organizations have a formal portfolio management department, the functions are still performed somewhere within the organization; for example, a vice president of finance and administration may serve as the portfolio manager. A manager of financial planning and control may, in fact, be performing many of the functions of a PMO but under another name.

4.2.4 Portfolio Management Process Interactions

The portfolio management function as related to the change life cycle framework is depicted in Figure 4-4. Portfolio management is most concerned with the definition and valuation of the results of a change initiative. The result of these changes, which are executed at the program and project levels, is also assessed on a continuing basis at the portfolio level.

Portfolio management may be classified as either tactical or strategic. Tactical portfolio management, like program management, addresses unique organizational strategies and objectives; however, in portfolio management, these unrelated projects and programs are often classified as subportfolios. Tactically, organizations need to work on the right projects, allocate resources in an optimal manner, and ensure projects are on schedule and on budget.

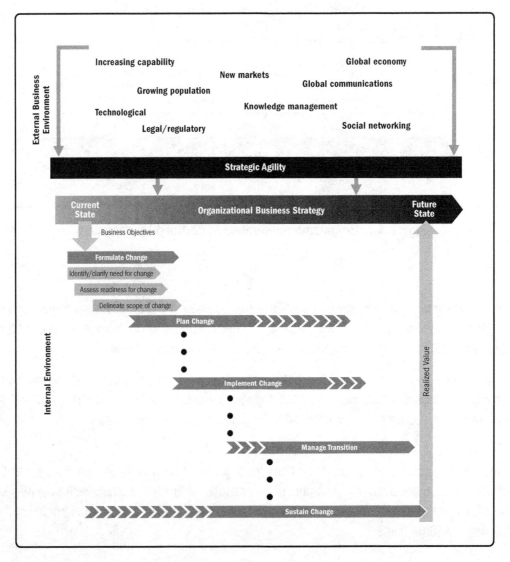

Figure 4-4. Portfolio Management in the Change Life Cycle Framework

At the strategic level, portfolio management is used to determine whether the selected projects, subportfolios, and programs align with the organization's strategies and realize the expected value for the business. The strategic portfolio is continually evaluated to determine whether the organization is undertaking the right initiatives based on its current strategy.

All subportfolios, programs, and projects involve some degree of change, spanning from minor or evolutionary change, such as the set-up of a new reporting system, to revolutionary change, (e.g., a merger with or acquisition of another company or replacing internal IT servers with a cloud-based solution).

4

When a strategic initiative requires significant changes in the organization, these changes are best addressed first at the strategic level. The following are examples of strategic initiatives requiring change management:

- Pharmaceutical company decides to enter a new drug category.
- Passenger rail organization decides to initiate high-speed rail service.
- University decides to add distance learning to its traditional classroom offerings.
- Software company decides to begin offering hardware that runs their software.
- Telecom company decides to outsource its facilities function.
- Federal agency decides to consolidate all regional planning on a central server.
- Trucking company acquires its largest competitor.
- Hospital needs to comply with rapidly emerging federal regulations.
- Country needs to reform and modernize a major agency.

The common thread in these examples is that all require significant change, which is best formulated initially at the portfolio level and then planned and implemented through programs and projects.

Organizations and people have a limit to their ability to absorb change over a given period of time. In the previous examples, it is possible that change may be such that the organization is stretched beyond its ability to absorb the degree of change required to execute the strategic initiative or initiatives. Frequently, in addition to dedicated program and project personnel, a significant contribution may be required from day-to-day operations personnel within the organization. When people are also asked to change the way they perform their work, three major factors come into play: (1) ability of the people to absorb the change, (2) potential resistance to the change, and (3) unintended impacts of the change (i.e., business process changes that could have a ripple effect on other organizational systems, such as finance, customer service, etc.).

4.3 Formulate Change

The formulation of the change through a portfolio of programs, projects, and operations begins with a thorough understanding of the strategic objectives. Stakeholder engagement with the strategy formulation team is critical for formulating the change initiative such that all aspects of the strategy are addressed in the change plan that leads to the outputs of the Defining Process Group discussed in Section 4.3.2.2.

4.3.1 Modify/Clarify Need for Change

4.3.1.1 Change Readiness vs. Urgency to Change

While senior executives in the organization may accept change management, there is a risk that the resulting decisions may not be accepted throughout the organization. Acceptance of portfolio management processes and decisions throughout the organization are required for portfolio management success.

Strategic goals always lead to change in the organization's people, processes, systems, and technologies. Not recognizing and formalizing the organization's ability to handle change may become a major obstacle to the full realization of the benefits expected from the portfolio.

Typically, for a fundamental change, organizational capability is assessed from the executive level to the operations level and includes key stakeholders. At this level, it is important to determine whether the organization believes it is capable of successfully implementing a new strategic initiative. A framework for exploring the level of urgency associated with the new strategic initiative versus the organization's perceived level of readiness to achieve it is shown in Figure 4-5. At one end of the spectrum, there is a lack of urgency and the organization is not ready to change (deliberately build capacity); whereas at the other extreme, the sense of urgency is great, and the organization is prepared in terms of the readiness of the systems and processes needed to successfully implement the required changes (fully prepared to act).

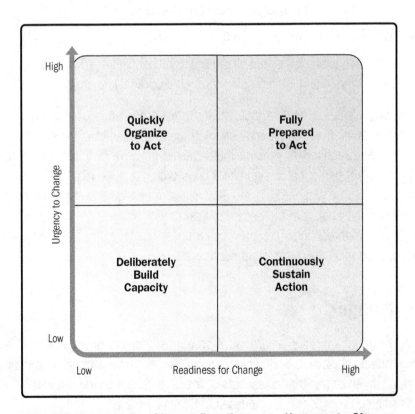

Figure 4-5. Assessing Change Readiness vs. Urgency to Change

The extent of change that the organization is able to accept is one factor used to determine the appropriate mix of portfolio components. This relates to the strategic objectives of the organization, which serve as inputs to the portfolio decision process. Each portfolio component should apply similar techniques to facilitate and handle change in a consistent manner.

Each quadrant indicates that there is a change capacity associated with it—either the organization needs to build the change capacity or take steps to sustain it. For example, with a new regulatory requirement, there may be a high degree of urgency to make a change, but preparedness for it may be low. The organization may respond to such a change by chartering a project with a crisis team to quickly determine how the organization needs to respond. On the other hand, if an organization's strategy requires building global capacity to expand its markets, the organization should proceed in a slow and cautious manner by chartering a program for the capacity-building effort. A key focus of this program is the change elements required to institute the structures, relationships, rules, policies, etc., associated with building and sustaining global capacity.

In an incremental, technical-level change, the assessment involves only the team affected by the change, but the assessment includes both the direct and indirect impact of the change on other teams or functions. For a change that affects an entire business unit or multiple business units, the functional managers and their teams are involved, and the assessment includes the capability of each section to absorb and integrate the change.

At this level, the focus is more initiative centered than strategy centric, because the readiness assessment determines how well the organization is positioned to effectively drive the initiative. Therefore, the change readiness assessment explores:

- **Governance.** Are the right leaders from across the organization involved in overseeing the initiative?
- **Sponsorship.** Is there an executive sponsor who is accountable for keeping the leadership, organization, and initiative aligned?
- **Accountability.** Is decision-making authority and responsibility assigned and at the right level?
- **Capacity to execute.** Are the resources required for the success of the initiative assigned and with the priority demanded by the initiative?
- **Failure and success.** Has the organization defined success and do people understand the consequences of failure?
- **Method.** Is the execution of the initiative structured using business methods that people understand how to apply?
- **Business case.** Are the benefits of the initiative clearly stated, measurable, and achievable?
- **Capacity to manage.** Once the initiative is executed, does the organization have the capacity to incorporate its outputs into sustained operational activities?
- **Resolve.** Will the organization see the initiative through to its conclusion with the full backing and support required for it to succeed?

Change readiness assessments include the capability for the affected section(s) of the organization to maintain a minimum acceptable level of performance during the change, because a change process usually impacts performance in the short term. Refer to Section 3 for more information on the various aspects of a change readiness assessment.

4.3.1.2 Communicating Strategic Intent

When extensive changes are indicated, the communication of strategic intent becomes increasingly challenging as shown in Figure 4-6. How deep into the organization the change needs to permeate varies from case to case. At times, strategic intent needs to be communicated through many layers of the organization to the actual front-line resource, shown at level 10, for example, "Establish a program to reduce customer service response time by 60 %." At other times, strategic intent is carried out at level 1, for example, "The position of Chief Strategy Officer is added to the executive team." Figure 4-6 summarizes four keys for transmitting strategic intent in the organization: (1) communications, (2) traceability, (3) transparency, and (4) accountability.

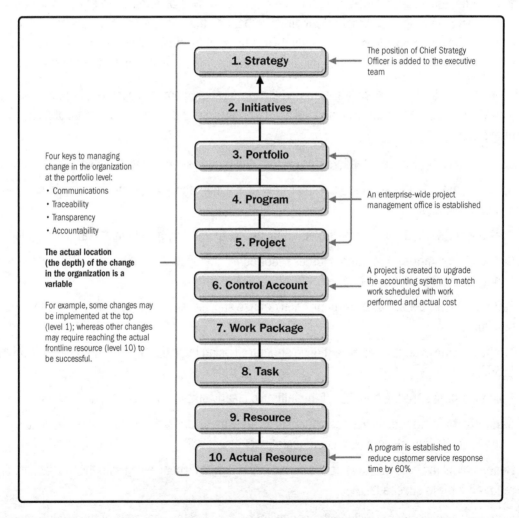

Figure 4-6. The Two-Way Communication Challenge from Strategy to Front-Line Resource

4.3.1.3 Change Management vs. Strategic Change

The degree of change management and strategic change contained in a portfolio ranges from "business as usual" in the lower left-hand quadrant to "bet the company" in the upper right-hand quadrant as shown in Figure 4-7. Each of the quadrants in the figure is described in Table 4-2.

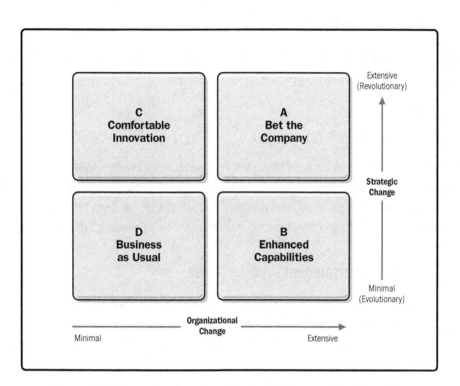

Figure 4-7. Organizational vs. Strategic Change in a Portfolio

Table 4-2. The Four Quadrants of Organizational vs. Strategic Change

A. Bet the Company	Extensive strategic change and extensive change management potentially provide the highest return on investment, but also are likely to be the highest risk. **Example:** An aircraft company undertakes a new aircraft development program requiring change management and strategic change. The change management focuses on outsourcing design of major components which has never been done before. The strategic change is to build the aircraft out of composite materials.
B. Enhance Capabilities	Extensive change management with minimal strategic change. **Example:** A decision is made to implement a project management office (PMO) across a geographically dispersed organization.
C. Comfortable Innovation	Extensive strategic change requiring minimal change management. **Example:** A decision is made to enter a significant new market. The existing organization is capable of supporting this new market initiative.
D. Business As Usual	Minimal change management and minimal strategic change. **Example:** The organization is in a commodity business with little opportunity or reason to use change management.

Strategy execution is generally not an all-or-nothing proposition. It is useful to think in terms of strategy realization. Research has indicated that high-performing organizations realize over 80 % of their intended strategy, while low-performing organizations generally achieve only a little more than 30 %. Strategy execution becomes more challenging as it increases on the *X* and *Y* axes (Table 4-2 provides additional detail).

4.3.2. Assess Readiness for Change

The Standard for Portfolio Management – Third Edition identifies three Portfolio Management Process Groups:

- Defining Process Group,
- Aligning Process Group, and
- Authorizing and Controlling Process Group.

These three Portfolio Management Process Groups do not have a beginning and an end like a project—they are cyclical. These three Process Groups are useful when (a) establishing the initial portfolio; (b) periodically updating the portfolio after it is established; and (c) a significant breakthrough or new discovery occurs, warranting a reevaluation of the existing portfolio and the possible development of a new strategic initiative.

4.3.2.1 Overview: Portfolio Management Process Groups

Managing portfolio-level change in the organization is explored within the framework of the Portfolio Management Process Groups as shown in Figure 4-8. It begins with the organization's vision and mission and ultimately yields performance and results. The additional detail on the actions contained within each of the three Process Groups is shown on the right side of the figure.

The three Portfolio Management Process Groups also interact with the inventory of work and organizational assets, such as portfolio process assets, organizational process assets, and enterprise environmental factors. The Process Groups have interdependencies and the portfolio manager utilizes these Process Groups in the management of each portfolio. Constituent processes can also interact both within their particular Process Group and with the other Portfolio Management Process Groups.

4.3.2.2 Change Considerations in Defining the Portfolio

The Defining Process Group shown in Figure 4-9 is most active at the time the organization identifies and updates its strategic goals, near-term budgets, and plans. Traditionally, these activities take place at the annual budgeting time although some organizations have more or less frequent cycles. However, significant changes in the internal or external environments may cause a reopening of the Defining processes at any time. Change management considerations for the Defining Process Group processes are listed in Table 4-3.

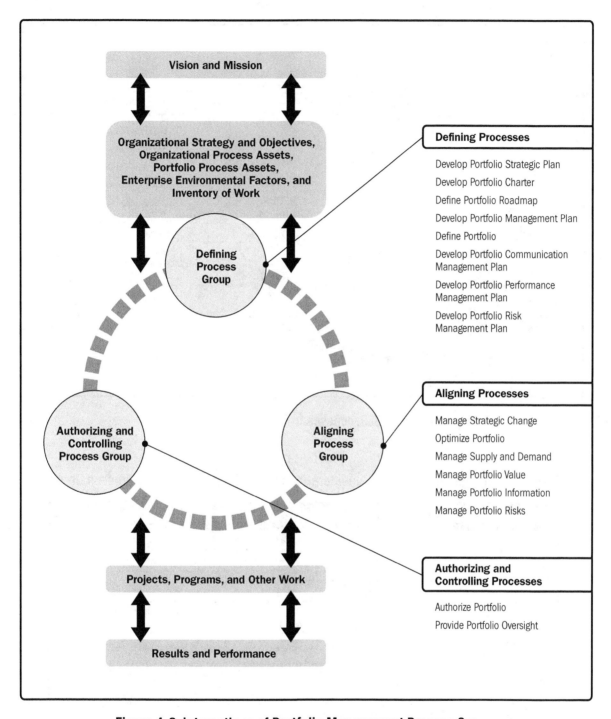

Figure 4-8. Interactions of Portfolio Management Process Groups

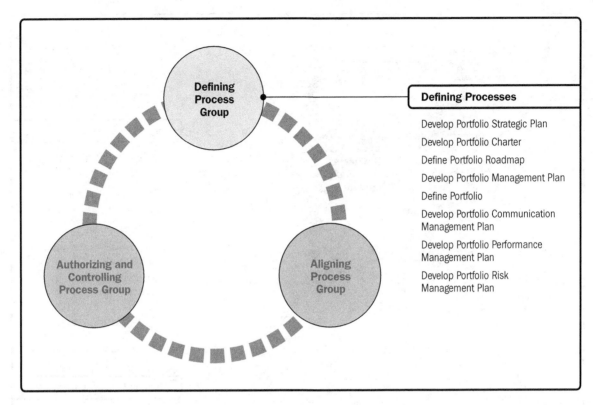

Figure 4-9. Processes in Defining a Portfolio

Table 4-3. Change Management Considerations in the Portfolio Defining Process Group

Defining Process Group	Change Management Considerations in Defining the Portfolio
Develop Portfolio Strategic Plan	The initial version of this plan will change and evolve before buy-in is received and when approval is sought from the key stakeholders, governing bodies, and portfolio managers.
Develop Portfolio Charter	The portfolio charter needs to account for both the organization's capacity to carry out the strategy and the environmental factors, which may be rapidly changing while the portfolio charter is written.
Define Portfolio Roadmap	The initial issue of this time-phased roadmap may require changes to reflect a growing understanding of the portfolio over time.
Develop Portfolio Management Plan	Incorporation of changes is an iterative process as subsidiary plans are developed.
Define Portfolio	The components of the portfolio may change over time due to factors such as availability, viability, and track record.
Develop Portfolio Performance Management Plan	This plan is essential to the tracking of deviations (changes) in resource capacity, resource utilization, and changing demand.
Develop Portfolio Communication Management Plan	This plan is designed to keep the stakeholders informed of the baseline strategy metrics and any changes that may occur during implementation.
Develop Portfolio Risk Management Plan	This plan establishes the risk strategy, tolerance, and thresholds.

4.3.2.3 Change Considerations in Aligning the Portfolio

The Aligning Process Group consists of processes to manage and optimize the portfolio as shown in Figure 4-10. The Aligning Process Group provides information regarding the strategic goals that the portfolio is to support, as well as operational rules for evaluating components and building the portfolio. The purpose of these processes is to establish a structured method for aligning the mix of portfolio components to the organization's strategy. Change management considerations for the Aligning Process Group processes are shown in Table 4-4.

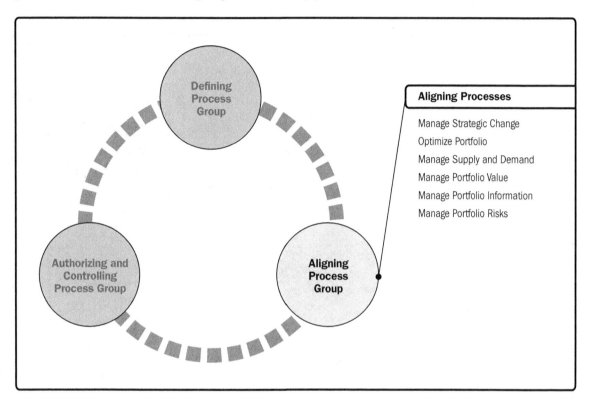

Figure 4-10. The Processes in the Aligning Process Group

Table 4-4. Change Management Considerations in the Aligning Process Group

Aligning Process Group	Change Management Considerations in Aligning the Portfolio
Manage Strategic Change	Change in the portfolio is a normal occurrence as strategy evolves from the current state to the future state.
Optimize Portfolio	Optimization of the portfolio is an ongoing process as circumstances change. For example, enterprise environmental factors may cause a strategic initiative to be delayed or canceled altogether.
Manage Supply and Demand	The changing of the availability of organizational resources versus the demand varies according to the organizational priorities.
Manage Portfolio Value	Managing portfolio value involves monitoring any changes in the expected value of the strategic components.
Manage Portfolio Information	Portfolio reporting represents a wide variety of inputs from multiple processes. The sources of these inputs are likely to change over the life cycle of the strategic component.
Manage Portfolio Risks	Risk planning is based on the known risks. Change and flexibility are required when a previously unknown risk surfaces.

4.3.2.4 Change Considerations in Authorizing and Controlling the Portfolio

The Authorizing and Controlling Process Group consists of the processes for determining how to authorize the portfolio and provides ongoing portfolio oversight as shown in Figure 4-11 and described in Table 4-5. These two processes are the activities necessary to ensure the portfolio as a whole is performing to achieve predefined metrics determined by the organization. These authorizing and oversight processes are very active parts of the portfolio and are ongoing functions of the organization's governing body.

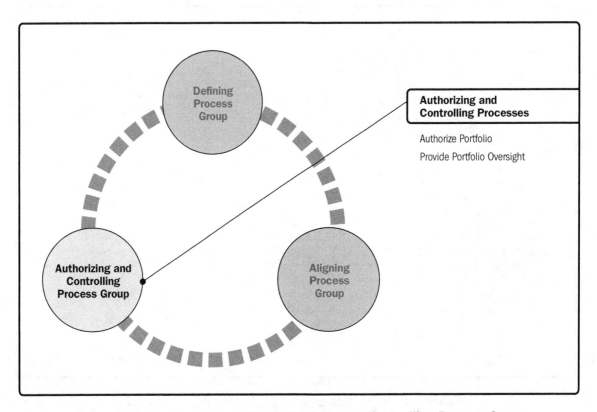

Figure 4-11. The Processes in the Authorizing and Controlling Process Group

Table 4-5. Change Management Considerations in Authorizing and Controlling the Portfolio

Authorizing and Controlling Process Group	Change Management Considerations in Authorizing and Controlling the Portfolio
Authorize Portfolio	Generally, changes to the authorized portfolio are introduced throughout the life cycle of the authorized components.
Provide Portfolio Oversight	Oversight involves monitoring the portfolio performance and recommending changes to the component portfolio mix, which may include the termination of previously approved projects that are no longer viable.

In cases where a high degree of change is required, oversight activities are particularly sensitive to indications of resistance to change. It is far more desirable to overcome resistance to change as early as possible, preferably before it occurs. Early intervention through education, communication, participation and representation, facilitation and support, and negotiation are some of the options available.

On the other hand, it is far less desirable to use change tactics such as cooptation, manipulation, coercion, and termination. Although resistance to change is typically part of the program management process, these activities may be required at the portfolio level with executive and strategic stakeholders, such as when an important component of the organization is skeptical and not yet on the team.

Resistance to change is frequently identified very early in the development of the Defining Process Group. In early identification, the portfolio communication management plan begins addressing how to facilitate the required change, as opposed to overcoming resistance to change at a later date, which is much more challenging. The following examples illustrate how early portfolio communication management planning leads to success.

- **Case study.** A large aerospace and defense contractor undertakes a major strategic initiative to move from project and program management to an enterprise-wide portfolio management capability. It was recognized in the early stages during the portfolio defining process that a major effort was needed to facilitate adoption of this organization-wide change. The company developed a comprehensive portfolio communication management plan that had the full support of the C-level executives. *Analysis:* Resistance was minimized through early and continuing education and communication.

- **Case study.** A major distribution organization simultaneously launched six strategic initiatives designed to reach a future state in several years. The President/CEO had an extensive project management background. Initiatives were built with inputs from all major stakeholders. The information technology department was already successful in using an early version of a portfolio server to manage all of the IT work. An enterprise program management office was established. Six senior program managers were recruited from within the organization to lead the six new initiatives. An extensive portfolio management plan was developed along with an innovative communication management plan, which combined all of the required factors to facilitate a smooth seamless integration. The organization moved from last in its category, according to business media, to first in its category for three consecutive years. *Analysis:* Success was attributed to a high level of maturity in organizational project management throughout the organization as well as a clear vision and the engagement of stakeholders from the start.

Fundamental changes in organizations frequently create a high-risk situation because insufficient time is allocated for impacted personnel to personally absorb the change. This rush to implementation may easily create conflict to a point where the entire portfolio is in jeopardy because critical subportfolios, programs, or projects are misaligned. It is the role of the portfolio management team to make sure that the time and resources allocated for the change are balanced with the ability of the organization to absorb and accept the change.

4.3.3 Delineate Scope of Change

The activity of defining the change management scope is similar to defining a project management scope, with the addition of the following inputs: change readiness assessment, change impact assessment, and agreements for coordination with program management. At the portfolio level, the scope of change is delineated at a high level. Additional elaboration of scope of change occurs at the program or project level as discussed in Sections 5.3.1.3 and 6.3.1.5.

4.3.3.1 Change Impact Assessment

Conducting a change impact assessment becomes increasingly useful as the combination of change management and strategic change increases in a portfolio. The impact assessment is designed to:

- Assist managers in evaluating and responding to change at the portfolio level.
- Ensure change is executed in the most efficient way possible and does not derail the effort.
- Increase strategy realization by monitoring and thoroughly understanding potential changes in the portfolio—its programs and projects.
- Alert the executive team when new information is discovered that can be leveraged to increase the likelihood of success.

The change impact assessment is designed to identify gaps in the organization's ability to successfully achieve the degree of change required to move from the current state to the future state. For the impact assessment to be useful to the executive team, identifying the existence of a gap is insufficient by itself. If the gap is significant, (i.e., it has the potential to reduce strategy realization) the executive team is likely to be interested in a remediation plan to close the gap.

The change impact assessment has two components: a gap analysis and a change readiness assessment.

- A change impact gap analysis is performed to compare the current portfolio mix and components with the change in strategic direction—an analysis essential to managing strategic change. This analysis determines the gaps between current capability and the capabilities needed to execute the new portfolio mix.
- A change readiness assessment is performed to assess how ready the organization is to perform the steps necessary to bridge the gap between the current portfolio state and the future state. The assessment determines the "if," "when," "what," and "how" of implementing the change and points out any capabilities not yet addressed that are required in order to effect the change. The change readiness assessment is described in Section 3.

To be most effective, the list of change impact gap analysis areas in Table 4-6 should be tailored to reflect the specifics of the organization, its culture, and its envisioned future state.

The change impact gap analysis and the change readiness assessment together build the change impact assessment. The change impact assessment is designed to improve the success rate for change management initiatives and to maximize strategy realization.

Table 4-6. Change Impact Gap Analysis

Sample Analysis
When evaluating the mix of initiatives in the portfolio:
• Determine the impact to existing systems. How will the portfolio changes interact with the existing systems? Will new systems need to be adopted and integrated?
• Determine the impact on the organization's processes. Review how processes are executed today versus what will be required with this portfolio.
• Determine the impact on the people of the organization. Are there changes in job descriptions and changing roles? Evaluate current role descriptions versus required levels of expertise.
• Determine the impact on the organizational structure. This analysis looks at both the organization chart as well as the physical structure (aspects of distributed workflow). Does the new portfolio create structures that provide diverse locations, outsourcing versus insourcing, or new partners, etc.?
• Determine the technology impact created by the portfolio. Does the new portfolio require changes to the technology infrastructure or acquisition of new technology?
• Determine the environmental impact created by the new portfolio. Look at the internal and external environmental issues including availability of capital, demographics of resources, and social and political issues.

4.4 Measure Benefits Realization

The purpose of a change initiative is to contribute to the organization's continued growth and sustain its competitive advantage. Successful execution of the change can only be measured through benefits realization, which is an assessment of the successful integration of the change into the portfolio, its programs, and its projects. Establishing expected benefits requires a systems view of the portfolio where each expected benefit is aligned with the vision and its contribution to the change purpose at the organizational level. The expected benefits and measures of success are set and aligned with the vision at the formulation stage.

Benefits realization is measured in a progressive way throughout the programs and projects contained in the portfolio. For this reason, intermediate and tangible benefits that are linked to the ultimate purpose, as well as the pace of delivery, are set during scope delineation, and the resources required to measure them are committed during the change planning phase. Each benefit is clearly tied to the overall strategy.

4.4.1 The Role of the Portfolio Manager in Measuring Benefits Realization

The portfolio manager may be an individual, a group, or a governing body responsible for establishing, monitoring, and managing all assigned portfolios. The portfolio manager initially facilitates exceptional, far-reaching plans for change management, then monitors the execution of the plan, and makes necessary adjustments along the way.

The role of the portfolio manager is further defined by considering the organizational change impact on the responsibilities shown in Figure 4-12.

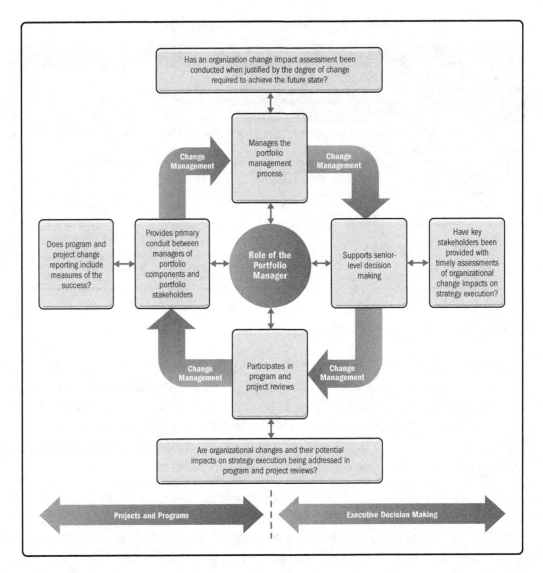

Figure 4-12. Overview of the Role of the Portfolio Manager in Managing Change in the Organization

The *Standard for Portfolio Management* – Third Edition states that the role of the portfolio manager may include the specific responsibilities shown in Figure 4-12. Each of these responsibilities may involve managing change in the organization.

Figure 4-12 graphically portrays the role of the portfolio manager in benefits realization and the routine and rigorous measurement of early indicators of change success: acceptance, adoption, and early results of the change and its benefits. The process of measuring benefits realization starts during the planning process and requires continuous attention from the portfolio manager, program managers, and project managers throughout the implementation of the change and the transition of outcomes into business operations. As depicted in the figure, there are four functions that the portfolio manager carries out with respect to managing change in the portfolio context.

- Supports senior level decision making by ensuring timely communication to stakeholders on progress.
  - Provides key stakeholders with timely assessment of portfolio component selection, prioritization, and performance.
  - Guides the selection, prioritization, balancing, and termination of portfolio components.
  - Influences active executive sponsorship engagement for the portfolio and each portfolio component.
- Participates in program and project reviews to reflect senior level support, leadership, and involvement in key decisions.
- Serves as the primary conduit between managers of the portfolio components and portfolio stakeholders.
  - Measures and monitors the value to the organization through portfolio performance metrics and targets.
  - Ensures ongoing alignment with evolving organizational goals and market opportunities and threats.
  - Provides early identification of (and intervention in) portfolio-level issues and risks that are impacting performance.
- Responsible for the execution of the portfolio management process.
  - Ensures the alignment with strategic goals and organizational priorities.
  - Assesses changes and impact on portfolio components.
  - Reviews, reallocates, reprioritizes, and optimizes the portfolio.
  - Establishes and maintains infrastructure and systems to support portfolio management processes.

4.5 Summary

Portfolio management supports change initiatives by assessing the current mix of portfolio components against the changes in organizational strategy set forth by the executive managers and by evaluating and adjusting the portfolio components based on measurements of benefits realization as each component is transitioned into operations. The portfolio manager carries out this function by:

- Supporting senior-level decision making through timely communications on progress;
- Participating in program and project reviews to reflect senior-level support, leadership and involvement in key decisions;
- Serving as the primary conduit between managers of the portfolio components and portfolio stakeholders; and
- Leading the portfolio management process in the organization.

In conclusion:

- Portfolio management is an ongoing management activity (subportfolios, programs, and projects have a beginning and end).

- Although a portfolio is typically deployed to represent a specific planning period, it is reviewed periodically in the context of a rapidly changing environment to ensure its continued relevance and ability to deliver intended business results.

- Accordingly, the mix of initiatives represented in a portfolio may undergo change over both the short and long term.

- As the portfolio is adjusted and those adjustments transition to the program and project levels, effective change management ensures the ongoing alignment and integration with evolving strategy across the organization.

- Ultimately the success of a portfolio is measured in terms of the aggregate investment performance and the realization of intended benefits of the organization's strategy.

5

CHANGE MANAGEMENT AT THE PROGRAM LEVEL

5.1 Overview

More and more organizations are coping with a complex and turbulent environment that requires them to address change as an intrinsic aspect of their management approach. As portfolio, program, and project management progressively develops as good practice for managing organizations coping with continually changing environments, change management is also becoming part of that good practice. Section 2 defines change management as a comprehensive, cyclic, and structured approach for transitioning individuals, groups, and organizations from a current state to a future state with intended business benefits. This section presents effective change management practice within the program management domain. It shows how program management, through its capability to deal with high levels of ambiguity and uncertainty and its focus on good governance, strategy alignment, stakeholder engagement, and benefits management, helps organization managers with the implementation of change strategies in a complex and turbulent world.

The purpose of this section is to emphasize good change management practices in program management.

5.2 Change Management in the Context of Program Management

Program management is increasingly considered a strategy implementation process. Unlike projects, programs do not have well-defined boundaries; both their beginning and end can be ambiguous. Ambiguity requires decision makers to be involved continually to make decisions as the program evolves through a series of cycles. This high uncertainty level requires the program team to continually seek accurate data so that stakeholders can make the right decisions. Due to its cyclic nature and its capability to address high ambiguity and uncertainty in a structured way, program management is ideally suited to deal with the complexity of change management.

Figure 5-1 displays the change life cycle introduced in Section 2 and emphasizes the scope of program management in relationship to change management. The relationship between change and programs is very close; many programs are now routinely used to manage organizational change and deliver strategies that involve changing the way organizations respond to their internal and external environments. Whereas the program management life cycle is closely linked to the change management life cycle, the change process covers stakeholder mobilization and engagement activities more in depth; it is also more subjected to ambiguity—the need to regularly review decisions and realign the process—than the more traditional technical or system programs. For details on the program management life cycle refer to *The Standard for Program Management* – Third Edition.

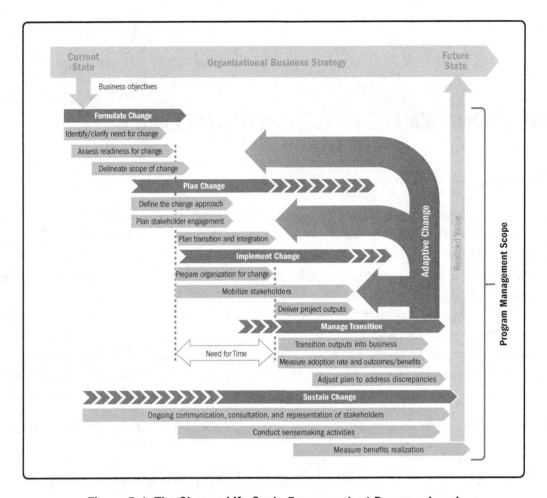

Figure 5-1. The Change Life Cycle Framework at Program Level

Section 2 of this practice guide describes each of the major steps in the change management life cycle displayed in Figure 5-1. This section compares the program life cycle with this change life cycle and outlines the similarities and differences between them (see also Section 5.2.3).

5.2.1 What is Program Management?

Whereas project management has evolved over the last 60 years, program management, as a discipline independent of project management, has only been developed in the past fifteen years. Program management evolved because (a) executive management wanted to better manage strategy implementation, and (b) the project management approach was expanded to encompass larger and more multifaceted endeavors.

The program and project management approaches were developed in parallel. The business community developed program management from a business viewpoint and focused on the strategic link of programs without really understanding the day-to-day processes required for effective delivery of tangible results. The project community attempted to regroup and coordinate projects to obtain benefits not available from managing them individually.

©2013 Project Management Institute. *Managing Change in Organizations: A Practice Guide*

Today, program management is characterized as the harmonized management of a number of related components through a common outcome or delivery of a collective set of benefits. Program management typically involves interdependencies between its components as well as the management of interfacing activities to increase synergy, coordination, and strategy alignment in order to deliver benefits for its stakeholders.

5.2.2 The Standard for Program Management

The Standard for Program Management – Third Edition clearly acknowledges the strategic and business link of programs and recognizes the need for programs to align with the strategy. The current standard also recognizes the need for business stakeholders to engage and to transition project results into operations in order to deliver benefits to the organization.

The Standard for Program Management – Third Edition also acknowledges the strong relationship between program management and change management; in particular the following sections directly address change activities:

- Section 2.3.2—Program Versus Project Change
- Section 4.4—Benefits Transition
- Section 4.5—Benefits Sustainment
- Section 5.3—Stakeholder Engagement
- Section 6.2.10—Monitoring Program Progress and the Need for Change
- Section 6.2.12—Approving Component Initiation or Transition
- Section 7 (The Program Life Cycle Management)—The program life cycle follows a similar approach to the change life cycle framework (see Figure 5-1)
- Section 8—Many of the program management supporting processes detail change management requirements and activities.

5.2.3 How Does Program Management Apply to Change?

The change life cycle has a similar structure to the program life cycle. Like change management, program management is a cyclic process that requires continual reevaluation in order to achieve its objectives. Change can be deliberate (planned) or emergent (unplanned) and usually the realized objectives are a mix of deliberate and emergent actions.

Program management is ideally suited to manage change in organizations because of its now well-recognized capability to deal with situations that are both ambiguous and uncertain. Table 5-1 compares the program life cycle phases described in *The Standard for Program Management* – Third Edition with the change life cycle framework introduced in Section 2 of this practice guide.

In the program environment, the need for change is viewed as an opportunity to respond adaptively to evolving circumstances and to ensure that the program remains positioned to deliver its desired benefits and value. This is especially true for organizational change programs that need to adapt to complex organizational and behavioral inputs.

Table 5-1. Relationship between Program and Change Life Cycles

Program Life Cycle Phases (The Standard for Program Management—Third Edition)	Change Life Cycle
Program Definition	**Formulate Change**
Program Formulation	Identify/clarify need for change
	Assess readiness for change
	Delineate scope of change
	Plan Change
Program Preparation	Define the change approach
	Plan stakeholder engagement
	Plan transition and integration
Program Benefits Delivery	**Implement Change**
Component Planning and Authorization	Prepare organization for change
Component Oversight and Integration	
(Continuous – Stakeholder Engagement[A])	Mobilize stakeholders
Component Transition and Closure	Deliver project outputs
Program Closure	**Manage Transition**
Program Transition	Transition outputs into business
	Measure adoption rate and outcomes/benefits
Adaptive Change[B] (at all phases)	Adjust plan to address discrepancies
	Sustain Change
Program Transition	Ongoing communication, consultation, and representation of stakeholders
	Conduct sensemaking activities
	Measure benefits realization
Program Closeout	

[A] Stakeholder engagement is not strictly a program life cycle phase; it is a continuous program activity that is a primary role for the program manager throughout the duration of the program.

[B] Adaptive change consists of all the activities required as the program adapts in response to environmental pressures, based on plan changes initiated by the program manager and integrator and authorized by the program governance board.

5.3 Change Management Practices within Programs

Program management is related to portfolio management and strategic objectives at the inception stage, and is related to operations and business as usual during benefits delivery and at the program conclusion. Projects are an intimate part of a program's deployment process. The purpose of program management is to harmonize the components (projects and other activities) and manage interdependencies along with transition in order to realize identified benefits that are aligned with portfolio and strategic objectives. Program benefits are measured in terms of organizational performance and results including business value realization and sustainable competitive advantage.

Although Figure 5-1 shows "sustain change" at the end of the change life cycle, good practice requires that the sustainment of change be supported by communications, consultation and representation, and sensemaking activities at the beginning of the process. Those activities continue until change is delivered successfully (see example given in Section 5.3.5).

Sensemaking is essential to successful change. The traditional response to complex situations is to gather information to reduce uncertainty, which may in fact increase confusion in an already complex issue. Sensemaking is an individual and group process that facilitates the resolution of conflicting perceptions and distinct expectations. Through its facilitating approach, sensemaking helps to clarify the impact of the change process and its results for each stakeholder. This is essential for finding the best approach and collectively acceptable solutions to the change process (see Section 5.3.5.2 for detailed sensemaking activities).

5.3.1 Formulate Change

Organizational strategy is a result of the strategic planning cycle, where the vision and mission are translated into a strategic plan. The strategic plan is subdivided into initiatives, of which programs are an integral part. Program formulation is the translation of the strategic plan into tangible objectives that are aligned with the stakeholder needs and expectations and define the program scope. In the case of change management, it is essential to understand and elicit the expectations of multiple and often disparate stakeholders to address any issues that they may have concerning the change process or its results. Program formulation also serves to define the pacing of change in collaboration with the recipients' representative, usually the integrator, in order to be able to mobilize the stakeholders and sustain the change.

5.3.1.1 Identify/Clarify Need for Change

In the context of an integrated OPM framework, the program team establishes the need for change and its contribution to continued growth and sustainable competitive advantage at the strategic and portfolio levels. The program team confirms the needs and expectations of the different stakeholders in order to reach agreement on the specific actions and outcomes of the program. In this context, the program team typically involves the program sponsor, program governance board, program manager and the integrator function, as well as key team members. The need for change should be clearly established at the strategic or portfolio levels before any other action is undertaken.

Elicitation of stakeholder needs is a key aspect of change programs. Stakeholder engagement is essential in any program; in change programs, the degree to which stakeholders are actively engaged is often directly correlated to success or failure. If the program team identifies needs and expectations of the stakeholders and achieves agreement or at least an acceptable compromise, success of the outcomes of the change program and its conversion into business benefits is likely.

As stated in *The Standard for Program Management* – Third Edition, program stakeholders cannot be managed, but their expectations need to be managed. Program stakeholders often have much more authority than the program manager or the program team. Therefore, stakeholder engagement is really a balancing act of the various program stakeholder interests, and the program manager and team assume a facilitating role rather than a directive role.

In change programs, the first step is to identify who the stakeholders are and map them to understand who they are in relation to the change. The program manager then determines what their interests and impact are on the program (see Figure 5-2 from *The Standard for Program Management* for an example of a stakeholder map). Once this is understood, the program team organizes workshops and/or interviews with the key stakeholders to understand needs and assesses their validity and alignment with the strategic objectives.

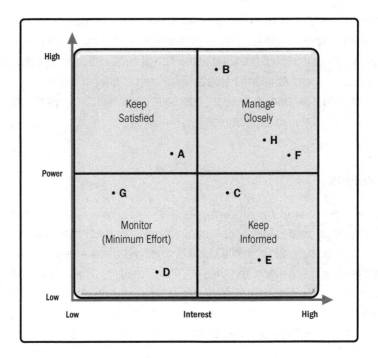

Figure 5-2. Stakeholder Map

The next step is to reach agreement on what the critical success factors of the change will be and how achievement will be measured. Many methods can be used to achieve this. Some examples of methods are described in Table 5-2.

All of these methods are used to obtain agreement of the group's goals and objectives and translate them into specific actions and measurable results to achieve objectives. These methods can be used concurrently and each group of managers will have their favorites. In a change program, the method is not as important as actively involving the key stakeholders in a group decision process.

5.3.1.2 Assess Readiness for Change

The identify/clarify need for change process (see Section 5.3.1.1) is used to gain agreement from the primary change stakeholders on the high-level objectives of the change. The next step is to set measures that are achievable and represent a true evaluation of the change results. However, before setting the measures, the program team needs to understand and consider its environment by assessing the organization's readiness for change.

Change readiness must be assessed from two perspectives (see Figure 5-2):

- The organizational systems (components) and structures (whole) that need to be improved or that will support the change (processes, procedures, physical facilities, and equipment); and

- The people (individuals) and culture (collectivity) that can support or resist the change.

Figure 5-3 is a simple graphical representation of these organizational elements.

Table 5-2. Methods for Measuring Program Benefits and Critical Success Factors

Method of Measurement	Program Benefits and Critical Success Factors
Value Management	A structured, multidisciplinary team decision-making process developed to increase the satisfaction of the needs of diverse stakeholders while optimizing the resources used to meet those needs. It is based on the use of functions (expected benefits) and the search for innovative ideas. It can be used for strategic decisions, portfolios, programs, and projects as well as for technical solutions.
Analytic Hierarchical Process (AHP)	A structured, group decision-making technique for organizing and analyzing complex decisions based on stakeholders' goals and their understanding of a situation. The technique consists of breaking down the problem and assigning weights to each component to help make the best decision.
Logical Framework	This technique is popular with international aid agencies and the UN. The logical framework describes four types of events that drive projects: activities, outputs, purpose, and goals. The objective is to create a logical cause–effect relationship between these elements to ensure that activities are linked to goals.
SWOT Analysis	Although the technique is mainly used to analyze the strengths and weaknesses of an organization or department, it is helpful to understand the context of the change and how the program can draw on strengths and mitigate threats and weaknesses to achieve opportunities.
Soft Systems Analysis	This method assumes that each stakeholder has a different view of reality and that these views should be discussed before reaching an agreement. Typically, it asks a group of stakeholders to build a new view that is agreed upon and then this view is compared to reality for identification of desired and feasible changes.
Strategy Maps	The strategy map is a framework based on the balanced scorecard concept. Its purpose is to elicit expected benefits on the basis of four major generic components: financial, customer, internal business processes, and learning and growth. It can be used in conjunction with other, more specific benefits-identification techniques.

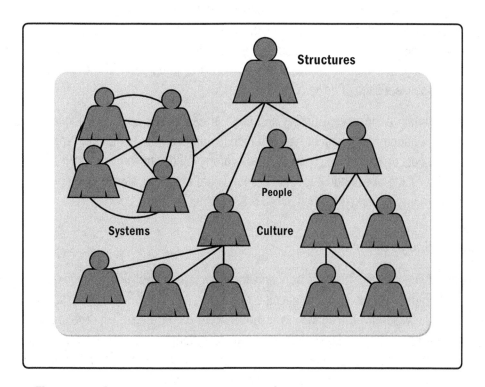

Figure 5-3. Organizational Systems and Structures; People and Culture

In both perspectives, availability of the right resources and prioritization of actions are essential aspects of success. The assessment should also include an evaluation of the impact of other change initiatives that are undertaken in, or impacting on, the organization and the organization's capability or capacity to absorb additional change. Even organizations that have a high capacity for change will have a tipping point and exceeding this tipping point could jeopardize the program even before it is undertaken.

Organizational systems should be considered in their entirety and not independently from one another. Generally there are many interdependencies between systems, and these need to be identified and harmonized. For example, a drop in project performance may require training, the development of standardized project management processes, the development or acquisition of a project management information system (PMIS), and a career development plan. All these initiatives then become program components and need to be developed concurrently. As program components, they are interdependent, for example, when the process is not defined before training is developed, or when the PMIS does not fit within that definition, the change will not produce the expected benefits, and resources will be wasted.

Existing systems can be synergists or inhibitors of change. For example, an effective enterprise data management system could help a team retrieve accurate and precise information about a department more quickly; a complicated procurement procedure could delay the hiring of subject matter experts to implement a change; a well-managed fleet could support the installation of a new plant in a remote area; a dilapidated and ill-maintained facility could hinder the installation of a new production system.

Another important aspect of change readiness is the capability of the existing organization to balance the speed of change, which is driven by the need to stay competitive and maintain production/operational performance during the change process. The integrator function (see Section 5.4) assesses the impact of the change on existing systems and, following this analysis, recommends a pace for the change. The integrator proposes any mitigating actions necessary to reduce negative impacts of the change process or integration of the change on the organization's performance and proposes a pace of delivery for the change.

The ability to maintain performance during a change is dependent on the willingness and capability of the people supporting it. Change management typically focuses on people and culture. Program managers are often responsible for this aspect of the change process and, therefore, need to be familiar with it so they can accommodate this function in their existing role or add it to another role. There are many aspects to engaging people in a change, and a number of them are presented in Section 5.3.5.2.

5.3.1.3 Delineate Scope of Change

As described in Section 5.3.1.1, when the need for change is established and the high-level outcomes are agreed on, the program team clarifies the specific outcomes of the change by classifying and prioritizing the change objectives. The vision for the change is established at the strategic or portfolio level and communicated to the program governance board. Stakeholders may hold differing views of the change process and specific outcomes. It is the role of the program team to create agreement on the change program objectives, confirm the ultimate purpose of the program, and translate the vision into specific outcomes.

This process generally involves three steps:

- Organize and prioritize the high-level objectives (critical success factors or CSFs) of the change program.

- Create measurable performance indicators (key performance indicators or KPIs) for each of the objectives.

- Clarify and agree on the specific outcomes and capabilities that the program will deliver and produce a document (roadmap or benefits register) that outlines them.

There are different methods used to organize objectives, for example, benefits breakdown structures (see Figure 5-4), hierarchical diagrams, and benefits maps. The purpose of this step is to create a hierarchy of the expected benefits or outcomes of the program that is aligned with both the strategic objectives of the change and the views of the key stakeholders of the program. Typically, the purpose/vision of the program is on the left hand side and is broken down into high-level benefits (CSFs), outcomes (KPIs), results, and capabilities by asking the question "How?" going from left to right at each level. The validity of the structure is verified by asking the question "Why?" proceeding from the right to the left. This how-why logic helps structure the benefit breakdown structure and create a strong link from the delivery of capabilities to the high-level strategic objective.

Once the different levels of the breakdown structure are agreed upon, the high-level benefits are prioritized in order to distribute resources effectively during the change process. Ideally, CSFs should number between five and eight, with a maximum of 12. Although managers often list more than that (up to 20 CSFs or more), criticality

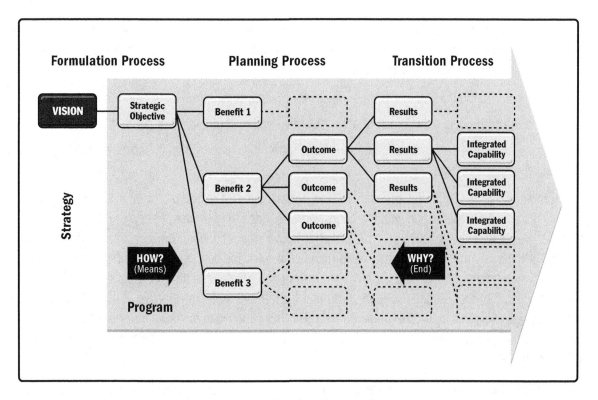

Figure 5-4. Benefits Breakdown Structure

diminishes rapidly as their number increases. The reason for prioritizing is to be able to optimize the use of resources by focusing the team's effort on actions that matter for achieving the objectives of the change.

There are three basic methods by which CSFs can be prioritized.

- **Simple rating system.** This system uses an alpha or numerical rating from one to five or one to seven to score elements from the most important to the least important.

- **Proportional voting.** In this method, participating stakeholders apportion a limited number of points (e.g., 10) to a number of elements. These elements are then classified in proportion to the total number of points that have been allocated to each of them.

- **Paired or pairwise comparison.** This technique compares a number of different elements in pairs to assess their relative importance to each other. Scores from the paired comparison are then summed up, and the resulting score permits the classification of the elements in order of importance.

When there is no objective data available, these three techniques are useful for comparing elements and prioritizing a small number of elements. Typically, in all three methods the score is presented as a percentage for clarity purposes.

Regardless of the selected method, it is essential to include all of the key change stakeholders in the prioritization process. The reason for this is very simple: when an influential stakeholder in the prioritization process is not included, decisions based on that prioritization are likely to be challenged.

Following the prioritization of CSFs, the program team sets clear measures of success for the change. Again, the team needs to involve the key stakeholders in the process that sets these measures. Some of the elements required to set a good measure of performance are:

- Define a criterion that is significant and actually measures what needs to be measured.

- Once the criterion is defined, set a target objective and acceptable range for that criterion.

- Define the measurement method and make sure it is achievable in terms of required resources, acceptability, and timeliness.

For example, when a CSF is set to "improve the performance of a group" through training, measuring the attendance at training or satisfaction with the course only provides the number of people who sat in on the course and whether they were either happy or not happy with the training; it does not measure how well they understood the material or the training's impact on their performance following the course. One way of measuring performance is to take a measurement of performance before the course and at intervals after the course to see if performance improved as a result of the training. However, note that if the training is not effective, it may be too late to make adjustments when using this method of measurement. Another option is to measure a sample group through a pilot course, make adjustments to the course based on these results and measure as the training is delivered to a wider and wider audience.

Change management takes time. Measures of success that provide immediate results (e.g., satisfaction with the training), may provide false indications of success; true measures of success are embedded into the change activities of the business and the actual realization of value for the organization. *The Standard for Program*

Management – Third Edition clearly defines the need for a benefits realization plan that formally documents the activities necessary for achieving the program's planned benefits and specifies the mechanisms that should be in place to ensure that the benefits are fully realized over time.

A roadmap for change includes specific elements, for example: (a) improve project delivery success from 65% within 15% of the planned schedule and cost to 75% within 12% of the schedule and cost; (b) increase production from 250 units per day to 285 per day; (c) reduce the incident rate from 12 per month to 4 per month; and (d) reduce time from production to market from 24 hours to 18 hours. All of these elements are based on actual measures of success, which are significant in that they actually measure the achievement of the change objectives and are within the capabilities of the program scope and resources.

Not all measures of success can be translated into financial terms; some measures of success may be associated with performance improvement, better working practices, or development of new capabilities. Although it is tempting to translate these measures of success into financial terms, sponsors should exercise care when taking a financial measure based on estimates and a set of factors that can change over time. For example, "time saved in a process" is often used as a measure for approving a change in working practices. Time saved is translated into FTE (full time equivalent) and multiplied by the number of employees to produce the scale of financial savings that an organization should expect through the change. This measure is flawed because it assumes that all employees will actually take less time to do a job and that the time they save will be used productively. Both measures are impractical, if not impossible, to verify.

Organizing and prioritizing high-level objectives, translating them into practical and significant measures, and putting processes in place to measure success all contribute to providing visible leadership for the change. Setting high-level targets linked to strategic objectives and measuring success, not only through financial, but also nonfinancial measures, requires a systems-thinking approach characteristic of current change methodologies and recent advances in change management.

5.3.2 Plan Change

Planning for change is different from planning for more product-oriented programs or projects. Although most programs contain elements of change and projects deliver results that are often linked to change, the purpose of some programs is to directly bring about change in organizations. Programs that deal with change are required to consider people and cultural issues as essential elements of the planning process (see Figure 5-5). Based on the analysis of the need and readiness for change, the program team sets the pace of delivery for the change.

The pace of the change is based on the progressive delivery of intermediate benefits until the ultimate purpose is achieved (see Section 5.3.4.2). The more fundamental the change, the shorter the change cycles will be, because the outcome is less predictable and needs to be reassessed more regularly. At the same time, the program will include longer transition periods and smaller change increments so that the organizational actors are able to integrate the change. A risk-averse organization may decide to deliver change in smaller increments; whereas an organization that accepts change and risk as part of its business may decide to deliver greater increments of change using longer cycles, because less predictability is required at the onset.

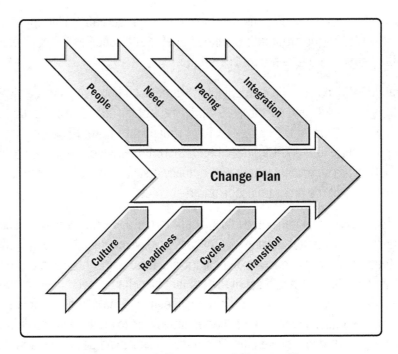

Figure 5-5. Influencers of Change Plan

Whereas projects are usually executed on the basis of an approved baseline plan, the planning of the program as a whole is an iterative process in which a baseline plan is only possible for the next cycle and an overall plan exists at the "educated guess" level.

All programs contain an element of change. For example, the following change elements are embedded in programs and are included as part of the program plan: (a) the need to engage stakeholders to support the program objectives, (b) the need to include transition and integration activities as part of the program, and (c) the measure of benefits at the operational level after the project outputs are delivered and being used.

5.3.2.1 Define the Change Approach

There are many well-known change approaches dating from the late 1940s until today. In most of these approaches, it is essential to hold a clear vision for the change and, in order to be successful, integrate the change into the organizational processes. The number and sequence of steps, type of leadership required, involvement of the different stakeholders, and focus and planning vary for each approach. Each organization is different and the approach used for a change program differs accordingly. These differences may necessitate that organizations adopt flexible approaches to adapt to circumstances and the degree of change.

The change approach affects the relationships among stakeholders. The manner in which the program team interacts with various stakeholders depends upon the following choices:

- **Number of steps.** The number of steps varies from one approach to the other. In organizations where change is easily accepted and there is a history of collaboration and empowerment, a few generic steps may be sufficient. In organizations where the culture is more traditional or structures are more elaborated, more detailed, specific steps may be necessary. The key is to match the change process to the organizational processes for purposes of increasing acceptance.

- **Sequence of steps.** The sequence of steps is another variable element. In some organizations and for more fundamental changes, it is essential to consult stakeholders and involve them from the start. In other cases, it may be possible to plan the change and conduct stakeholders' consultation activities while the change is implemented.

- **Type of leadership.** The type of leadership varies from authoritarian to democratic or even laissez faire. The choice of leadership style is based on a number of factors: (a) when the change is fundamental, more democracy is needed, (b) when speed is required for short-term results, it may be necessary to exert more authority, and (c) when the organization has strong social networks and is generally self-organizing, laissez faire may be the right choice. In addition, in power-distant cultures, authoritative behavior is expected and respected and may be a more effective approach for any type of change.

- **Involvement of various stakeholders.** Fundamental strategic change requires direct and continuous involvement of the executive level of the organization, whereas more concrete, specific change or operational level improvement requires more involvement of lower-level supervisory personnel.

- **Focus of change.** The focus of the change determines what type of process is more appropriate. For incremental changes at the process or technique level, a simple, more specific process may be required; whereas for fundamental strategic changes, an elaborate change process that involves multiple stakeholders from different levels of the organization may be required.

- **Planning.** Planning of the change process is dependent upon the complexity and turbulence of the environment. In a complex and turbulent environment, the change cycle is shorter and involves a smaller proportion of the scope for the change because predictability is lower. In simpler, stable environments, the cycles are longer and encompass a larger portion of the scope because results are more predictable.

The change process illustrated in this section integrates the program management life cycle described in *The Standard for Program Management* – Third Edition with the change process described in Section 2. The success of the change process is not viewed as the realization of the baseline plan, but as the capability to respond effectively to an evolving environment. Therefore, the plan should allow for feedback, adaptive change, and parallel rather than sequential activities. Key aspects of a good change management plan are responsiveness and openness to emergent inputs.

The program plan is a translation of the vision into specific outcomes. The program plan is the overall documented reference by which the program will measure its success throughout its duration. It should include metrics for success, methods for measurement, and a clear definition of success. This is typically the responsibility of the program manager and, in a change program, is accomplished in close collaboration with an integrator. The program governance board is also involved in an executive role. In a change program, the program manager and integrator consult extensively with the recipients, adopting a facilitating rather than a directive role. In addition to the program vision, mission, goals, and objectives, the program plan includes a roadmap and an environmental assessment. It also identifies the measures for change adoption and benefits realization.

The expected level of performance for the organization during the change transition cycles determines the pace of change. Change should be integrated so as to prevent performance from dropping to an unacceptable level.

Although change can be integrated on an ongoing basis, planners will include transition activities at the end of each cycle and plan for periods of stability where change is absorbed by the organization. These are inputted into the roadmap to define the end of various projects that deliver results in each cycle.

The program roadmap defines the milestones of the program, including the success criteria and results that should be delivered at each milestone. It clarifies the links (interfaces and dependencies) between program activities and expected benefits. The roadmap is a high-level view of the program process and should include major change facilitation activities. The program monitoring and appraisal process is built around the program cycles that are identified in the roadmap.

From a change program point of view (see Figure 5-6), the project elements that need to be monitored are:

- **Review milestones,** corresponding to deliverables that directly contribute to benefits;
- **Interdependency activities,** affecting the interface between the projects within the program; and
- **High-level tasks,** grouping the project tasks corresponding to the delivery of a measurable result.

In addition, the planning phase includes the conclusions of an environmental assessment that analyzes the internal and external elements that may impact the program process or results. In a change program, the identification and assessment of environmental influences is especially important because change programs are more complex than "physical systems" programs and more subjected to adaptation during the course of the life cycle.

Finally, the plan defines measures of change adoption and of benefits realization. Traditional project management measures project results; however, in a change program, the measure of success is based on the integration of the change into the business to improve competitive advantage. This requires setting measures as described in

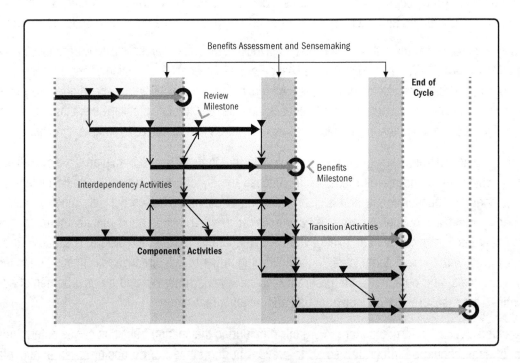

Figure 5-6. Roadmap Elements

Section 5.3.1.3. In change programs, the program team (a) establishes intermediate measures to demonstrate progress toward objectives, and (b) includes measures of the ultimate success of the change process. These usually correspond to the milestones defined in the roadmap, and both elements of the plan need to be integrated.

5.3.2.2 Plan Stakeholder Engagement

One of the distinct aspects of both program management and change management is the concept of distributed control. Traditional organizations and projects rely on directive control; however, because of the involvement of multiple stakeholders of varying degrees of authority, programs and change distribute control by empowering the people that are part of the process.

When multiple stakeholders are involved, different views are considered and agreed upon when making decisions to generate new ways of working. These decisions may concern new work practices and processes, new products, or simple process improvements; however in all cases, a number of concerned stakeholders are consulted and represented in the decision process. This approach requires that staff from all levels of the organization be empowered to make decisions at their level of authority.

While operational and administrative improvement is a continuous process that is easily acceptable because of its evolving nature, change creates a discontinuity in known patterns of behavior and work and is more difficult to accept. Top-down programs deal with clearly stated objectives and well-defined structures, requiring the program manager to play a coordination role because most stakeholders assume a more passive role. Change requires an open management approach to allow the program manager and other stakeholders to maintain active roles in defining specific goals and objectives from more abstract strategic concepts.

The primary objective of stakeholder engagement, as defined in *The Standard for Program Management* – Third Edition, is to gain and maintain stakeholder buy-in for the program objectives, benefits, and outcomes. Stakeholder engagement also includes negotiation of objectives, agreement on benefits, commitment to resources, and ongoing support throughout the program. The standard further states that it is the role of the program manager to spend extensive time and energy with all known stakeholders to ensure all points of view have been considered and addressed.

The key point in this phase of the change process is to assess the potential for support or resistance to the change and to develop a stakeholder engagement plan considering the following aspects:

- Organizational culture and acceptance of change,
- Attitudes about the program and sponsors,
- Expectation of program benefits delivery,
- Degree of support or opposition to the program benefits, and
- Ability to influence the outcome of the program.

5.3.2.3 Plan Transition and Integration

The Standard for Program Management – Third Edition clearly outlines the need for transition activities as part of the program process. This is a recent evolution triggered by the fact that program management is used more and more to manage organizational change. As stated in Section 5.3.1.3, change cannot be achieved through the delivery of results and new capabilities alone, but requires that these results or capabilities be used by the organization to produce benefits and value. This requires implementation of transition activities at the component and program levels. The responsibility for transition and integration is usually shared between the program manager and the integrator function.

Transition includes all activities necessary to achieve the ultimate program objectives. In a change context, transition and integration cover a number of activities that are softer in nature, for example, information and decision meetings, interviews, and workshops in addition to communication, training, coaching, and consultation. One important aspect of change is to provide enough time to absorb the change. This requires the right scheduling and sequencing of delivery activities and the preparation of the people and systems for the new reality. The data collected from the change readiness assessment is used to plan the transition and integration of the change.

The complete change plan, but in particular the transition, is based on agile concepts. It favors responsiveness as the measure of value in addition to the following actions:

- Delivering business results regularly to foster support and motivation,
- Responding to change in order to allow for evolutionary and adaptive development,
- Focusing on people and interactions to create harmony and allow for ideation, and
- Collaborating with and representing customers through stakeholder engagement.

This means that the change program plan will not look like a traditional project plan, but will have provisions for emergent activities. Typically in a change program, the team is able to predict accurately the expected results of the next cycle, but the results for the following cycles are estimated as accurately as possible with the data available at the time and adjusted on the basis of the results achieved in previous cycles (see Figures 3-5 and 5-4). The length and frequency of the cycles depend on the degree of outcome predictability. The higher the complexity and/ or turbulence, the lower the predictability and the shorter and more frequent the cycles.

There are numerous shared principles between agile management and change programs. For example:

- The objectives of the change program plan satisfy the customer through early and continuous delivery of valuable benefits.
- The program team views changing requirements as opportunities to increase the customer's competitive advantage.
- The governance board creates a collaborative and mobilized team of agents and recipients.
- People are trusted to get the job done and make the right decisions based on level of authority.
- Regular team meetings are promoted.
- Progress is measured through tangible results.
- Reporting and control systems are kept as simple as possible.
- These systems promote iterative and cyclic processes based on the impartial assessment of results.

5.3.3 Implement Change

As explained in Section 5.3.2, a change plan's baseline evolves continually and needs to be revised on an ongoing basis. This does not mean that the vision needs to be continually revised (i.e., if it was well defined at the start, it should stay consistent throughout); it means that the detailed processes for the vision can be adapted to changing circumstances. This explains why the planning, implementation, and transition processes are overlapping as shown in Figure 5-1, and why the overall change process consists of a series of cycles. (See Figure 5-6 and Section 5.3.4.2.)

This section examines the implementation of one of those cycles, but also looks at the overall process. The implementation process is closely linked to the other change processes because it is through implementation that new capabilities will be delivered for the organization. Assessment for change readiness, including planning for transition and integration, were addressed in the two previous sections. These activities prepare the organization for change and are iterated during implementation to adjust for any discrepancies. The stakeholder engagement plan is the basis for mobilizing the stakeholders during the change and sensemaking activities conducted in the sustain change process, which are directly influenced by the need to mobilize. Finally, the delivery of project outputs addresses the needs that were identified in the scope delineation and the measures of adoption that were agreed upon and will be measured—not only at the project level—but at the program level when benefits are realized.

5.3.3.1 Prepare Organization for Change

Preparing the organization is primarily a part of the integrator function (see Section 5.4). This function analyzes the sensemaking activities required to facilitate the change (see Section 5.3.5) and reports results to the program team, in particular to the program manager.

During formulation and planning, the integrator identifies areas of resistance and support and regularly monitors evolution in both resistance and support before the change process begins.

Resistance to change is not necessarily negative but is often the manifestation of dissatisfaction with the solution rather than with the change itself. When indicated, the integrator and program manager should meet with the resisting parties to discuss their issues and to find an acceptable solution.

When support for the change is identified in the business, the integrator should identify the people who are positive toward the change and recruit them as agents to actively promote the change in their functional area and report back any issues that should be addressed by the program team.

In order to prepare the organization for change, the program team initiates reinforcing activities and projects including transition and integration activities. These program components were identified in the planning phase of the program. Each component is initiated at the appropriate time in the program and integrated to incorporate its output to the program as a whole. Preparing the organization for change also requires the program team to identify and take into account influences from the program environment. These influences can be internal to the organization or come from external sources. Figure 5-7 is a graphical representation of this process.

Finally, the program team should ensure that all of these actions are aligned with the vision and strategy of the program and with the organization's goals.

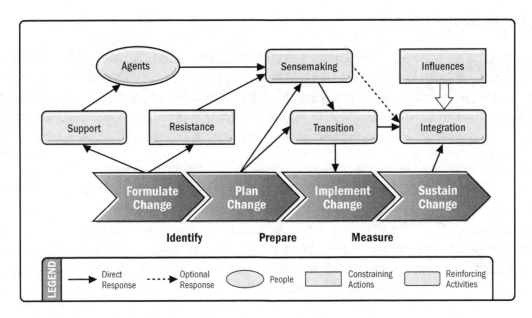

Figure 5-7. Primary Integrator Functions

5.3.3.2 Mobilize Stakeholders (Recipients and Agents)

Mobilizing stakeholders is an obvious issue in any program, but difficult to accomplish. One of the best methods for mobilizing stakeholders is to empower staff through distributed control; however, this requires a cultural approach that organizations may be reluctant to consider. In order to empower employees and team members, the latter should be made aware of the ultimate objectives and purpose of the change. Team members should be empowered to make decisions within their function's responsibility and be able to actively participate in higher-level decision processes creating "transforming" exchanges where they can influence outcomes.

In a change process, the program team needs to consider that agents and recipients will adapt continually to new circumstances and, therefore, new sensemaking activities may need to be undertaken on a regular basis to keep them mobilized. The program team should organize meetings where agents from different functional areas discuss specific issues and try to find common-ground solutions. These meetings can serve to flag unresolved issues between functional areas as well as possible synergies.

For example, the technology and operations department of a large financial institution decided to implement a change program to become a project-based organization based on OPM principles. As the program progressed, the operations personnel displayed more and more resistance to the change until their agent was able to determine that the term "project-based" was the problem. The operations people were feeling inferior to the project people. The agent suggested changing the name of the program to "value-based organization." The modification was immediately accepted and supported by operations personnel.

Stakeholders' influence may also change over time and, besides monitoring key stakeholders on a regular basis, the program team may need to undertake specific activities to maintain ongoing support. Ideally, the delivery of change benefits on a regular basis assists stakeholders to understand progress toward the organization's objectives. The program team ensures that these benefits are measurable, tied to the stakeholders' needs and expectations, and useful to them, even if only partially. In that sense, this is a flexible process.

Finally, the program team specifically responds to any resistance or apathy from the various stakeholders as well as to management pressures to accelerate the change process when it is best to take time for sensemaking. In order to address this issue, the program team refers to the pacing for change that was set during the change planning stage and reconsiders it when necessary, while adding the required transition or integration activities to make any change of pace successful.

5.3.3.3 Deliver Project Outputs

Project outputs are in the form of products, services, and results (outputs, outcomes, or documents). Programs deliver benefits, and benefits can only be obtained when project results are used. The project (or project phase) closure usually includes transition activities as described in *A Guide to the Project Management Body of Knowledge* (*PMBOK® Guide*) – Fifth Edition. When projects are part of a program, the program team coordinates these activities in order to achieve the program objectives and align with strategy. The program team, when applicable, will undertake the transition activities that are not part of the project scope.

From a program point of view, the project outputs need to be assessed, not only on their intrinsic merit, but also on their contribution to the change process and expected business benefits. Benefits can be measured only when the project deliverables are integrated into the operational processes.

Project outputs deliver new capabilities for the business and are assessed against the needs of recipients and fit. These needs may change during the course of the program and even during the course of a project. The satisfaction of the various stakeholders with regard to project deliverables is measured at the time of delivery, not in relation to the baseline. It is not the project result that is important for the organization, but rather its integration into the business to realize value.

5.3.4 Manage Transition

Change cannot be successful without a transition process. The transition process is what links the program with the operations side of the business and business as usual. It incorporates measures that will enable the organization to sustain change in the longer term. The transition process deals with the interdependencies between project deliverables and the rest of the business. It integrates the delivery of results with their adoption as new capabilities or work processes. Successful transition is what the measure of success is based upon and what will enable the business to potentially realize value in the long term.

At the program level, transition involves a system's view of the change where all the elements interact in real time to create new networks and patterns within the organization. As components of the change are released into the business, people's relationship to the system as a whole changes, frequently generating emergent inputs that require the program team to react and implement unplanned activities to deal with these emergent inputs.

Some reorganizations may require reconsideration or realignment of the entire program. Such realignments are labeled "adaptive change." This type of program-level decision is typically done at phase-gate reviews under the authority of the program governance board. The program manager is responsible for replanning and integrating project results and changes in the program direction.

5.3.4.1 Transition Outputs into Business

The program manager, in collaboration with the integrator, monitors the integration of the component project outputs into the business. This joint activity assesses the delivery of business benefits and value, which are measured against the key performance indicators that were set during scope delineation and are stated in the benefits register. Benefits are assessed on a continual basis and are measured as detailed in Section 5.3.5.3.

Successful transition and integration confirm success of the change effort. During the change process, as project results are being delivered, an ongoing transition process occurs to integrate the new capabilities into business as usual. The progression and sequence of transition activities are determined by the pacing of the program benefits, which were determined at the planning stage.

Transition activities are based on an understanding of the organization's culture and structure, which is part of the change readiness assessment (see Section 3.4). Transition activities should be part of each project's scope or, when unable to be associated directly to a project, should be considered program activities. These activities should have a scope, budget, timeframe, and responsible party including expected results.

Transition activities can also be used to take corrective measures or realign action when necessary. For example, in the event that the program manager realizes that training does not measure up to expectations, it may be possible that work conditions are not conducive to the new capabilities. The program manager and integrator can set up new procedures to match the training received or accelerate a parallel standardization project to implement new standards quicker than originally planned.

The transition process is underlined by flexible methods—the continual need to deliver working results, consult with stakeholders, and readjust as the change process progresses.

5.3.4.2 Measure Adoption Rate and Outcomes/Benefits

Measure results at the business level—not in terms of product results, but in terms of performance results (see Figure 5-8). For example, a training program that is part of an organizational effort to increase project delivery performance cannot be measured by the number of people that have been trained or their satisfaction with the training.

Examples of true measures of success are:

- **In the short-term.** Acquisition of knowledge, measured by knowledge assessment before and after the training;
- **In the medium-term.** Knowledge transfer or application of training to work, measured by the conformance to new performance standards, for example, use of a reporting system or tools and techniques demonstrated in the training; and

©2013 Project Management Institute. *Managing Change in Organizations: A Practice Guide*

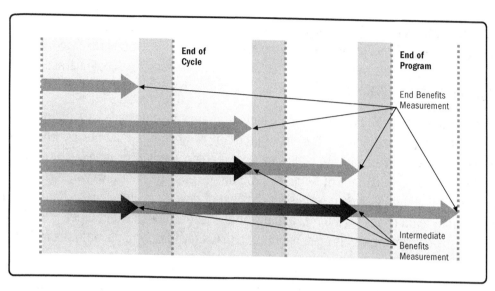

Figure 5-8. Planning and Measuring Intermediate Benefits

- **In the long-term.** The ultimate measure of success is an improvement in overall performance. However, this is often difficult to measure accurately because a direct cause-effect relationship between training and performance cannot be clearly established, and over time, other factors come into play. This difficulty in measuring results in the long term is exacerbated when management is reluctant to wait for the measure of long-term results and will not commit to it.

These examples show the importance of having measures of success that can be assessed at different stages of the change process in order to show progress toward the stated objectives. None of these measures assesses the product—they measure the transition of the product (training) into the business (increased knowledge, change or work practices, and individual and organizational performance).

It is not sufficient to measure the actual performance results of the change process. The ultimate objective of change is to sustain competitive advantage, and competitive advantage is often a matter of adapting to a changing environment or developing new opportunities quickly. So in any change program, the measure of the rate of change integration becomes a key aspect of success. During formulation and planning, the program team sets the pace for benefits delivery to the business. It is against that plan that value is assessed, keeping in mind the balance between the need for speed and the need to maintain performance during the change process.

The ultimate goal of any change process is to deliver maximum value to stakeholders. It is easy to focus on sponsors and business stakeholders when measuring outcomes and benefits, but the program team, supported by the program governance board, needs to account for all of the stakeholders involved if the change is to be successful.

5.3.4.3 Adjust Plan to Address Discrepancies

Adaptive change is an integral part of the program management process. Adaptive change is triggered by the fact that programs typically have a high degree of uncertainty and ambiguity. Whereas uncertainty is linked to turbulence and speed of change, ambiguity is linked to complexity and the existence of multiple possible options. Uncertainty management requires known project management techniques like work breakdown, planning, estimating, and risk management. Ambiguity requires more flexible methods like continual stakeholder involvement, sensemaking, and reviewing objectives to adapt to emergent inputs.

In program management, and particularly in change programs, discrepancies are not necessarily measured against a baseline plan, because the full suite of program components may not be known in the program definition phase. The program management plan and roadmap document the intended direction and benefits of the program. However, at the component level, the program is replanned iteratively at the end of each cycle on the basis of emergent inputs, delivered results, integration of new capabilities, and changes in direction. This requires the program team to assess internal and external changes in context in order to understand how they impact the program deployment and its components and how they affect the ultimate realization of the program objectives.

Aside from adding, eliminating, or realigning program components, replanning may involve slowing the pace of change to accommodate resistance or the need for additional sensemaking, or accelerating it to cope with external pressures for faster intake of the changes.

5.3.5 Sustain Change

Sustaining change starts as soon as the readiness for change is agreed upon and the scope is defined. Many change programs or projects fail because they do not take this aspect into consideration and view the change as a sequential process. An example of good practice is the recent multi-billion dollar change program in a government department that was in operation for more than 100 years and employed over 100,000 people. In this fundamental change program, the program team started conducting sensemaking activities 20 weeks in advance of any change implementation to ensure support from recipients.

Sensemaking is an important change concept; it allows different actors who are part of or subjected to the change to each make sense of the situation. Ideally, the recipients build a collective understanding of the situation, develop an agreed-upon strategic model of the process, and define a shared outcome. Sensemaking activities are a crucial part of any change process and start as soon as the need for change is acknowledged. Often, resistance to change is caused by a lack of sensemaking time. In addition to resistance, the promoters of change need to address apathy or overenthusiasm, because both can jeopardize a successful integration of the change.

As the change process progresses, the program team needs to measure its success. As stated in the previous sections, the success of any change process lies in the benefit realization value for the organization and its stakeholders. Measures of success are set during the formulation and planning of the change and measured on a regular basis during the life cycle and at the end to ensure that the objectives have been achieved. These measures, when taken on a continuous basis, provide the program team with an accurate assessment of the resistance or acceptance of the change.

Benefits sustainment is an important aspect of program management that is specifically covered in Section 4.5 of *The Standard for Program Management* – Third Edition.

5.3.5.1 Ongoing Communication, Consultation and Representation of Stakeholders

Communications and consultation are covered in Section 5.3.3.2. One aspect that needs to be clarified is the concept of "representation." Representation is different from simple participation because it involves active participation in a decision-making process in comparison to being present when the decision is being made. *The Standard for Program Management* – Third Edition states that stakeholder engagement is more than communication and its main objective is to gain stakeholders' buy-in for the program's objectives. Representation requires decision makers to empower other stakeholders to provide input and agree on decisions. It requires a two-way communication process as well as consultation with the stakeholders. This requires an organizational culture that is open to change and ready to empower its recipients to facilitate a successful implementation.

Another important aspect of change management that distinguishes change programs from technical programs is the need to define change management approaches beyond a simple process approach. Section 5.3.2 covered planning the change process and outlined the need to select or develop a change approach appropriate for each situation. The choice of change approach is dependent upon the culture and structures of the organization as well as its organizational processes. Known change processes have many things in common, but their application varies in several ways, in particular with regard to the following aspects that affect communication, consultation, and representation.

- Strong leader's role vs. decision making through a steering group (coalition),
- Passive communication vs. active communication,
- Simple attendance vs. dynamic contribution,
- Focus on systems and procedures vs. people and interactions focus, and
- Baseline implementation plan vs. adaptive change.

Each change situation may require a different approach, and each of these aspects needs to be addressed by the program team in order to select the best methodology. Each of these aspects of the change process influences the way the program team communicates, consults, and encourages representation of the stakeholders.

5.3.5.2 Conduct Sensemaking Activities

Sensemaking consists of conversational and social practices that enable individuals and groups to make sense of what is happening around them. Sensemaking may be formal or informal and verbal or nonverbal. Activities like gossip, discussions, sharing experience, rumors, social networking, and others are frequent sensemaking practices in organizations.

In a change process, sensemaking activities consist of the organized individual and collective activities necessary for the stakeholders to build an understanding and acceptance of the impact and outcomes of the change process and agree on its expected outcomes. These activities are related to the engagement and mobilization of stakeholders during a change process and include both management approaches and specific activities. Such activities include, but are not limited to, the following:

- **Sensemaking management approaches:**
  - ○ Clarification of vision and strategy,
  - ○ Empowerment of stakeholders,

- o Acceptance of innovative ideas,
- o Tolerance of ambiguity,
- o Distributed control (dependent on existence of communications and networks),
- o Open communications,
- o Development of social networks (not digital networks, but rather the way people connect with each other), and
- o Motivational and engagement activities (teambuilding and others).

- **Specific sensemaking activities:**
  - o Networking,
  - o Individual interviews,
  - o Team meetings,
  - o Information meetings,
  - o Decision meetings,
  - o Facilitated workshops,
  - o Coaching and mentoring, and
  - o Training.

The purpose of these approaches and activities is for the agents and recipients to be able to assimilate the impact of change with the least possible disruption. One aspect that will be discussed further is the need to maintain an acceptable level of performance during the change, which requires a fully functional staff.

Sensemaking is only effective when it is a flexible process where results are measured regularly both at the performance and acceptance levels, and corrective measures are developed with input from the recipients. Some human factors are difficult to measure; however, managers and agents have a tendency to be overoptimistic and not rely on actual measures before taking action.

5.3.5.3 Measure Benefits Realization

The ultimate purpose of change is to contribute to the organization's continued growth and to sustain its competitive advantage. Successful execution of the change can only be measured through benefits realization, which is an assessment of the successful integration of the change into business as usual. Setting benefits requires a systems view of the program where each expected benefit is aligned with the vision and its contribution to the change purpose at the organizational level. The expected benefits and measures of success are set and aligned with the vision at the formulation stage.

Benefits realization is measured in a progressive way throughout the program. For this reason, intermediate and tangible benefits that are linked to the ultimate purpose, as well as the pace of delivery, are set during scope delineation, and the resources required to measure them are committed during the change-planning phase. Each

Strategic Objective	Benefits	Projects	Business Expectation/ Measure of Success
Respond to new market position (Build new facilities and relocate 1,200 employees)	Change organization while maintaining work culture	Relocate 1,200 employees over 18 months	Reduce resistance and adaptation period
		Hire new employees (included in 1,200)	Minimize culture integration period
		Redesign jobs and reengineer business	Encourage acceptance of new systems
		Introduce new IT and networking systems	Methodology accepted by most personnel
	Deliver fit for purpose buildings in timely manner	Balance facilities delivery with workflow	Pace delivery to BAU requirements
		Deliver facilities to required standards	Delivery according to requirements
		Coordinate construction with operations	Minimize workflow disruption
	Maintain productivity...		

Figure 5-9. Executive-Level Benefits Register Example

benefit is clearly tied to a critical success factor that is aligned with the overall strategy through a benefits map, which was covered in Section 5.3.1.3.

In order to measure benefits realization, the program team should build a benefits register that enables them to measure the progress of the change and enables the program governance board to report on progress at the executive level. During the implementation of the change, progress will be measured against this benefits register. The benefits register includes two types of activities: (a) project activities that deliver specific results, and (b) transition activities based on the acceptance of the new capabilities that have been delivered and their successful integration into ongoing business practices.

Benefits registers are used to report to the executive level where benefits are identified in qualitative terms, or may be used as a program management tool. When used as a program management tool, the measurements are quantitative and refer to specific results. An example of an executive-level benefits register is shown in Figure 5-9.

Programs are typically longer term than projects and may evolve as they are executed. The program team and governance board are able to use the program's achievement of intermediate benefits as a means to market the program's progress to agents and recipients in order to obtain their continuous support and motivate them.

5.3.6 Specific Change Management Activities in Program Management

Table 5-3 outlines the specific change management activities that program managers need to be aware of when managing a change program.

Table 5-3. Identification of Specific Change Activities throughout Program and Change Life Cycles

Program Life Cycle	Change Life Cycle	Specific Change Activities
Program Definition	**Formulate Change**	
Program Formulation	Identify/clarify need for change	Analyze internal and external pressures Define purpose/vision Identify and classify stakeholders
	Assess readiness for change	Assess impact of change on business Assess business capabilities and staff receptivity Map stakeholders (positive or negative interest and power) Identify potential agents
	Delineate scope of change	Agree on critical success factors and key performance indicators Prepare benefits map and benefits register
	Plan Change	
Program Preparation	Define the change approach	Choose a change process adapted to structures and culture
	Plan stakeholder engagement	Prepare for sensemaking Identify specific activities to mobilize and engage stakeholders
	Plan transition and integration	Identify transition and integration needs in collaboration with integrator Identify transition and integration activities
Program Benefits Delivery	**Implement Change Process**	
Component Planning and Authorization	Prepare organization for change	Initiate sensemaking activities Identify areas of resistance and support Initiate transition and integration activities Initiate support activities and projects
Component Oversight and Integration		Ensure that project results are fit for purpose and well transitioned
Ongoing Stakeholder Engagement	Mobilize stakeholders	Empower agents and recipients Conduct sensemaking activities
Component Transition and Closure	Deliver project outputs	Assess fit for purpose Assess results integration into business as usual
Program Closure	**Manage Transition Process**	
Program Transition	Transition outputs into business	Assess delivery of business benefits and value Take corrective or realignment action if necessary
	Measure adoption rate and outcomes/benefits	Assess rate of change integration
Adaptive Change	Adjust plan to address discrepancies	Assess internal and external changes in context Readjust pace of change according to needs Initiate corrective actions if needed
	Sustain Change	
Program Transition	Ongoing communication, consultation, and representation of stakeholders	Identify external and internal influences Define change management approaches Monitor for resistance and/or apathy Respond to resistance and/or apathy
	Conduct sensemaking activities	Implement specific sensemaking activities
	Measure benefits realization	Assess integration of change Identify realized benefits Market the program
Program Closeout		

5.4 Organizational Capabilities in the Program Management Context

Organizational capabilities need to be assessed at two levels (see Section 5.3.1.2):

- The organizational systems and structures (processes, procedures, physical facilities, and equipment); and
- The people and culture aspects.

Systems and structures can be assessed objectively, but need to be monitored on a frequent basis to assess the pace and amount of change to ensure successful long-term integration of the change. The objective of this assessment is to make sure the performance of the organization or department stays at an acceptable level during the change process and increases after the change. It is expected that performance will drop temporarily during a change, but minimum acceptable levels should be set as part of the planning process, and this drop in performance should be limited in time.

People and culture are aspects of change management that are essential to success, but more difficult to control objectively. The key to success lies in the constant collaboration between all the stakeholders involved in the change process. The program governance board and, in particular, the sponsor(s) and integrator(s) are integral in support of the program team.

During the program change process, the program team works closely with the sponsor (executive or group of executives) to continually clarify and align the vision of the program and its ultimate purpose. Together, they confirm that the necessary resources are committed to the program and that the organization is ready for the change. This typically involves the appointment of an integrator function that is also represented on the program governance board. The integrator function can be fulfilled by a management-level employee from the department where the change occurs, an employee from human resources, or an external consultant; but whoever provides this function needs to have a thorough understanding of the organizational culture.

The integrator works in close collaboration with the program manager and the program sponsor to prepare the organization for the change and to ensure that the performance of the organizational department(s) affected by the change will not drop below an acceptable level during and after the change process. The integrator is generally represented on the program governance board and, as such, has both organizational insight and decision-making authority.

Integrators may accomplish some of the following tasks:

- Clarify new capabilities that are delivered as part of the change initiative,
- Assess the impact of the change on existing capabilities,
- Analyze the capability of the organization to integrate the change(s) both structurally and culturally,
- Identify the structures necessary to support the change,
- Agree on the pace of change for the program,
- Prepare recipients for change (knowledge, skills, and attitude),
- Alert the program team to any passive or active resistance to change,
- Assess the need to decrease or accelerate the pace of change, and
- Finalize any residual implementation of change once the program is closed.

5.5 Summary

Program management is similar to the management of change in terms of the high level of ambiguity and uncertainty and many of the activities that take place in a program are associated to the management of change. Some specific change activities need to take place when a program directly addresses organizational change, for example, sensemaking activities and the management of agents and recipients. The involvement of an integrator contributes to a successful transition and integration of the change into the business-as-usual activities of the organization. In conclusion, it may be said that the application of program management to the management of change, and particularly organizational change, will help organizations to integrate and align people, processes, structures, culture, and strategy.

The next section examines the impact of change on project management. Although most projects are part of a program, others may be managed as stand-alone endeavors. In that case, some of the activities covered in this section apply to the management of projects.

CHANGE MANAGEMENT IN THE PROJECT MANAGEMENT CONTEXT

6.1 Overview

This section covers how change management impacts the management and outcomes of projects, and helps to define, plan, obtain resources, and monitor critical change management activities as part of project plans. This section reviews the most important factors for consideration when delivering successful change through projects:

- Change that is reasonable, measurable, and capable of being sustained over a long period of time;

- Thoughtful planning to address risks in the fluid environment of change and the limitations in controlling those risks;

- Capability of the project team to carry out and integrate all supporting activities that impact the delivery of project benefits;

- Importance and challenges of communications, stakeholder participation, and monitoring/responding to potential resistance;

- Proactive monitoring, adjusting, and reworking of project plans to optimize the intended outcomes;

- Effective coordination with program management activities, recognizing that the activities of change management most often extend beyond a single project.

6.2 Change Management in the Context of Project Management

Change management in project management is a balancing act between boundaries and controls on the one hand, and fluidity and adaptation on the other. Because change is iterative and continuous, implementing change through time- and scope-bounded projects can be challenging.

Project managers are tasked with ensuring that projects transition from a current state to a future state and that the intended business benefits are realized by integrating and aligning people, processes, structures, culture, and strategy—all elements of the definition of change management (see Section 2). Project managers need to consider the following:

- **Project's role in benefits achievement.** The focus in change management is on the achievement of business benefits. This outcome cannot be achieved by the project's deliverables alone. However, when viewed from a change management perspective, the project manager is responsible for ensuring that the intended business benefits will be achieved through the project's results. When applying change management, the project manager's goal is to deliver change that has been adopted (integrated into the organization's work), and to ensure that the intended benefits are on track to be delivered operationally over time.

- **Project's adaptive responses to change in the environment.** Change that occurs during the course of a project is assumed to be a predictable occurrence and requires continual reassessment of plans. This assumption of frequent reactive change in the environment is further explained in Section 2. The *PMBOK® Guide* states "Due to the potential for change, the development of the project management plan is an iterative activity and is progressively elaborated throughout the project's life cycle." Change management places emphasis on looking for sources of potential change in the project environment, and uses adaptive techniques in the planning and implementation of a project's deliverables. When change is viewed as a predictable part of the project environment, a change management plan shifts from an emphasis on control to an emphasis on continued, cyclic review and adaptation.

- **Project team's supporting experts.** The scope of activities and skills required on a project team adds complexity and extends the project's scope. The *PMBOK® Guide* suggests that supporting experts may be engaged as part of the team, for example, in contracting, financial management, logistics, legal, safety, engineering, testing, or quality control areas. Change management suggests the need to plan these activities in the development of new policies, job descriptions, reporting structures, managerial activities, operational performance measures, regulatory reporting procedures, and others. While these are operational activities, the success of the change is dependent on planned and monitored actions to define, implement, and integrate them; and supporting capability may need to be added to the team.

- **Project's scope of activities in relation to the program scope.** Project activities (e.g., new policies, job descriptions, reporting structures, managerial activities, operational performance measures, regulatory reporting procedures, etc.) can be handled in three ways:

  ○ *As part of a program plan,* where the program defines specific projects (e.g., a specific project outlined in the program plan to create, review and integrate all job descriptions), and the program integrates the projects along with others that interact with deliverables;

  ○ *As activities to a project or projects having other deliverables* (e.g., defining job descriptions and work processes specifically for the delivery of a new customer service system), where the program retains accountability for integrating the project deliverables into an operational transition during program closeout; or

  ○ *As discrete project activities,* either delegated by the program manager or the project sponsor, where all change management activities are included as part of the project.

  Therefore, the boundaries between program scope and project scope require particular clarity in project-initiating activities and occasional reclarification when defining stakeholder needs and requirements. The project manager and program manager need to communicate and coordinate information, issues, and activities.

- **Project's attention to human factors outside the project team.** Change management provides a process for addressing human emotions and motivations, which are displayed during the course of implementing a project. When stakeholder engagement plans and communication management plans are included as part of the program management plan, the project manager becomes involved and the project's stakeholder management plan needs to consider engagement and communication activities that may be separate from or extend the activities included in the program management plan.

6.2.1 What is Project Management?

The *PMBOK® Guide* – Fifth Edition defines a project as "a temporary endeavor undertaken to create a unique product, service, or result," and further notes "most projects are undertaken to create a lasting outcome." In order to create a lasting outcome, project management activities need to be assessed continually for their ability to deliver not just an intended deliverable, but an intended deliverable that effectively supports the creation of a lasting outcome.

The *PMBOK® Guide* – Fifth Edition defines project management as "the application of knowledge, skills, tools, and techniques to project activities to meet the project requirements."

Change management focuses on the less tangible aspects of transitioning to a future state in order to achieve the intended business benefits. It helps to integrate project management activities into a process that contributes to a lasting outcome by extending the knowledge, skills, tools, and techniques available to project managers to performance of project management responsibilities.

6.2.2 The Standard for Project Management of a Project

The Standard for Project Management of a Project (Annex A1 of the *PMBOK® Guide*) defines the process, techniques, and guidelines commonly used in the practice of project management.

Some change management practices are implied in the *PMBOK® Guide*, but specific descriptions are not included due to the wide variety of change management practices in existence today. This section of the practice guide identifies good practices associated with the integration of change management into project management practice.

6.2.3 How Does Project Management Apply to Change?

Project change management activities span all phases in the change life cycle framework shown in Figure 6-1 (and introduced in Section 2), depending upon the project's scope of activities defined in 6.2. When a project is not part of a program, there is a direct interface with portfolio management during the Formulate Change activities. Usually project change management activities begin during the Plan Change phase. Plan Change activities may be a function of program management, project management, or both, and require coordination between program and project management activities. Projects are concerned with the Implement Change and Manage Transition life cycle phases. All projects need to perform elements of Sustain Change as part of their activities. More importantly, project activities continually adapt to meet changing needs in the implementation and transition of change, as represented by the feedback arrows in Figure 6-1. Major activities in this change life cycle of a project are offered in more detail in Section 6.3.

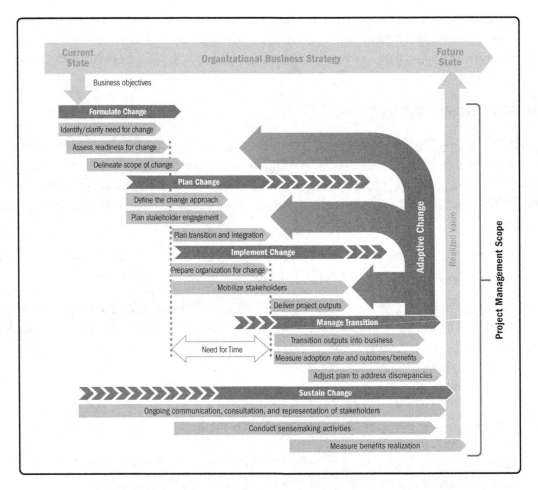

Figure 6-1. Change Life Cycle Framework—Project

Recognizing the interaction between program and project management in the change life cycle is a critical factor for implementation of a change program or project. Coordination of change management activities in program management and project management are shown in Table 6-1, which was first introduced in Section 5 to show the interaction of change management in program management.

All change management activities are executed in the course of project management when the project is not part of a program. More often, change management activities will be undertaken both in program and project management, with those performed in project management becoming more detailed and coordinated through program management.

Table 6-1. Coordination of Program, Project, and Change Processes

Program Life Cycle Phases (The Standard for Program Management—Third Edition)	Project Management Process Groups (PMBOK® Guide —Fifth Edition)	Change Life Cycle
Program Definition		**Formulate Change**
Program Formulation		Identify/clarify need for change
		Assess readiness for change
		Delineate scope of change
Program Preparation	Initiating and Planning[A]	**Plan Change**
		Define change approach
	Planning[A]	Plan stakeholder engagement
	Planning[A]	Plan transition and integration
Program Benefits Delivery		**Implement Change**
Component Planning and Authorization	Planning	Prepare organization for change
Component Oversight and Integration		
(Ongoing Stakeholder Engagement)	Executing	Mobilize stakeholders
Component Transition and Closure	Executing	Deliver project outputs
Program Closure		**Manage Transition**
Program Transition	Executing	Transition outputs into business
	Monitoring and Controlling (when explicitly part of project scope)	Measure adoption rate and outcomes/benefits
Adaptive Change (at all phases)	Monitoring and Controlling (when explicitly part of project scope)	Adjust plan to address discrepancies
Program Transition		**Sustain Change**
		Conduct sensemaking activities
		Measure benefits realization
	Monitoring and Controlling	Monitor for resistance and/or apathy

[A] If the project is not part of a program, the planning of the project is undertaken during the "Plan Change" process. If the project is part of a program, it is undertaken during the "Component Planning and Authorization" of the program.

6.2.4 Change Management Activities in Project Management Process Groups

Key change management activities are viewed in the context of Project Management Process Groups. Table 6-2 represents some of the key intersections and considerations when integrating project management and change management.

In the remainder of this section, the change management activities described in Table 6-2 are correlated to the change management processes shown in Figure 6-1.

Table 6-2. Change Management Activities in Project Management Process Groups

Initiating Process Group	Planning Process Group	Executing Process Group	Monitoring and Controlling Process Group	Closing Process Group
Identify lead and other resources Identify stakeholders and their vested interest in the change Coordinate change management activities and program management change activities Delineate change management scope Begin change communication	Collect change management requirements and define change management scope Define, sequence, obtain resources and budget change management activities Identify measures of benefit realization Clarify risks to change acceptance and adoption, and plan abatement activities Develop communications management plan, human resource management plan, and quality management plan	Acquire and organize change management team, including procuring outside resources, when applicable Manage change communications	Assess change acceptance Review and modify change management scope, activities, project schedule, and project budget based on acceptance assessment feedback	Measure change acceptance/adoption against established measures Identify, plan, and execute actions needed to transition the change into business operations Close out the project with a plan for sustainability

6.2.5 Change Management in Project Management Knowledge Areas

Another way of summarizing how change management overlaps with project management is to view it with regard to the Project Management Knowledge Areas as shown in Table 6-3.

6.3 Change Management Practices in Project Management

This section covers change management activities that represent good practice in project management. These activities follow the change life cycle framework (Figure 6-1), and elaborate on the activities specifically mentioned in Table 6-2.

6.3.1 Formulate Change

In general, project managers are not involved in this step of the change life cycle, although, as stakeholders, they should have access to information pertaining to project planning.

- Completed change readiness assessments (see Section 3.4) are used to determine the scope of change management activities pertaining to risk.

- When projects are not part of a program, the project manager works directly with the portfolio manager and the sponsor to develop a scope for the project and determine the needs for change management activities.

In change management, portfolio and program management typically address the Formulate Change activities. To the extent that there may be touch points in project management, they are addressed here.

Table 6-3. Change Management and Project Management Knowledge Areas

Knowledge Area	Project Management Emphasis	Expansion Implied in Change Management
Project Integration Management	Managing interdependencies and unifying project components	• Managing and unifying interdependencies with change management activities performed in program management • Ensuring transition of project deliverables into operations for ultimate achievement of project, program, and strategic benefits
Project Scope Management	Clarity and limitation of scope	• Soliciting input into scope before agreeing on limitations • Planning scope as new information or challenges develop
Project Time Management	Completion of a project on a schedule	• Building adaptive and iterative processes into the schedule
Project Cost Management	Estimating, funding, and controlling costs	• Ensuring realization of expected business benefits with project deliverables having reasonable cost structure
Project Quality Management	Ensuring quality of deliverables	• Ensuring that quality deliverables result in expected business benefits
Project Human Resource Management	Organizing, leading, and managing the project team	• Ensuring and coordinating change management resources and activities for the project
Project Communications Management	Communicating project information to stakeholders	• Seeking participation of stakeholders in communication • Delivering extensive two-way communications
Project Risk Management	Planning for and controlling risks to project scope, schedule, and budget	• Planning for and monitoring risks, particularly those posed by peoples' actions and reactions • Adapting project deliverables and outcomes, as necessary, to ensure realization of expected business benefits
Project Procurement Management	Planning for, securing, and controlling contracts for products or services necessary to complete the project	• Planning for, securing, and controlling contracts for services necessary to ensure change adoption and ultimate realization of expected business benefits • Obtaining professional expertise in such areas as process design, organization design, and knowledge transfer, when applicable
Project Stakeholder Management	Engaging stakeholders in defining expectations; analyzing, negotiating, and managing expectations	• Engaging broad range of stakeholders when defining expectations • Seeking stakeholder participation in decision making • Testing stakeholder assumptions

6.3.1.1 Identify/Clarify Need for Change

When a project is part of a change program, clarification of the need for change is well developed and stated as part of the project charter. If a project is not part of a change program, Section 5 covers the required activities to ensure clarification is accomplished before the project charter is completed.

In the *PMBOK® Guide*, the process of developing the project charter consists of clearly defining the project start and project boundaries. Although the project management team may assist in writing the project charter, according to the *PMBOK® Guide*, the business case assessment, approval, and funding, which are part of the Initiating Process Group, are handled outside of the project boundaries.

The Initiating Process Group processes set the vision for the project and clarify what is needed to successfully deliver the project outputs. The Initiating processes align stakeholders' expectations with the project's purpose and encourage stakeholder participation to ensure that expectations are achieved. The *PMBOK® Guide* defines project stakeholder management as the creation and maintenance of relationships between the project team and stakeholders to satisfy needs and requirements within the project boundaries.

When projects are conducted in a change context, project managers may need to accomplish tasks beyond the typical project boundaries. Ideally these additional tasks should be part of the agreed on project scope to ensure successful delivery of the change; otherwise, the project manager should alert the project sponsor and request a scope change.

6.3.1.2 Identify Lead and Other Change Management Resources

Change management activities should begin early in the definition of a project; therefore, the people leading the activity should be established and defined in the project charter.

The lead (see Section 2.2.3) for change management activities may be the project manager, the program manager, integrator, sponsor or a dedicated employee. The specifics regarding the lead function are coordinated or managed in an organizational project management environment as discussed in Section 3.

The lead function is generally responsible for planning and coordinating execution of the following change management activities in a project (when not planned and executed as part of program management):

- Communication with stakeholders, including participation in decision making and mobilization toward adoption of the changes;
- Process design and redesign;
- Organizational design (e.g., reporting structures, management of new/changed organizations);
- Identifying and establishing measures for acceptance and substantive adoption of the change; and
- Identifying, planning, and adapting plans to address risks, such as resistance to change.

Once the lead is identified, the lead may identify additional change management resources, based on results of the change readiness assessment and project scope definition. Remaining activities in this phase are carried out by the lead.

6.3.1.3 Identify Stakeholders and Stakeholder Expectations in the Change

The *PMBOK® Guide* provides good direction for identifying project stakeholders, and is the starting point for change management activities specific to stakeholder identification.

Change management stakeholder identification requires a greater analysis of each primary stakeholder group to better understand potential areas of risk to the acceptance and full adoption of the change, for example:

- Who and what may influence acceptance and ultimate adoption of the change;
- Secondary and tertiary potential stakeholders whose influence on project success may be tangential but important (for example, the perceptions of a labor union may influence employees); and
- Degree of volatility in stakeholder positions on the change.

In change management, there are more *external* stakeholders than typically defined in a project. As stakeholder interests and influences are identified, this information is added to the stakeholder register. When addressing change management risks, it is useful to add the following information about stakeholder points of view regarding the change to the stakeholder register:

- How the change benefits each stakeholder (from the stakeholder's perspective);
- What assumptions each stakeholder is making about outcomes of the change; and
- What losses each stakeholder incurs as a result of the change (e.g., status, influence, work environment (i.e., less desirable work hours or location), relationships, income potential, etc.).

It is also useful to add a judgment about the *volatility* of each stakeholder or stakeholder group's support for the change—*what* could alter a stakeholder's support for a change and its outcomes, *how easily* that influence could change the stakeholder's support, and *to what degree* the support may be withdrawn. For example, a change in the opinion of a key customer related to the change may create significant volatility in the sales organization's support for the change. In general, when the number and strength of the influencers are greater, the volatility of support for the change from an individual or group is also greater. Where there is great volatility, it is useful to prepare multifaceted stakeholder management and communication management plans.

6.3.1.4 Coordinate Change Management Activities with Those Done in Program Management

Change management activities begin before traditional project chartering and encompass a broader range of activities; therefore, some or most of the activities are managed at the program level. Coordination of responsibilities and schedules for the change management activities between process owners is important when developing the project scope. When activities related to benefits definition and measurement, communications, process design, organizational structure design/redesign, and training are involved, the following types of questions should be addressed.

- Who is planning and scheduling these activities? How will this project be incorporated at the program level? How will resource constraints be handled?
- When planning and scheduling is performed at the project level, how will project activities be incorporated into the program management plan without overlap or confusion?
- Who is responsible for monitoring and adjusting communication, training, or processes based on feedback, new issues, etc.? How will resource constraints be handled?
- How will the program and project manager handle changes that impact only the project, or both the project and program, which may require a larger or different audience or plan?
- How are benefits defined and measures developed for determining the success of the change? How will change success (i.e., acceptance, adoption, and initial results) be defined, assessed, tracked, and addressed through changes to program or project scopes, schedules, or resources?

6.3.1.5 Delineate Scope of Change

The activity of defining the change management scope is similar to defining a project management scope, with the addition of the following inputs: change readiness assessment and agreements for coordination with program management.

Clarity regarding the following change management priorities is important to include in the project charter:

- Plan for, monitor, and address risks that affect the acceptance, adoption, and sustainability of the change to ensure benefit achievement. Planning for these risks is covered more thoroughly in Section 6.3.2.1.

- Define high-level measures of success and needs of the project team to establish methods for measure and to adapt project results throughout the project.

- Incorporate actions into the project management plan, which are needed to transition the project outcomes into sustainable business operations.

- Include outcomes in the project charter, which are useful in coordinating change management.

- Keeping in mind that change management should ensure a level of change adoption takes place before project closeout, include information on success criteria and approval requirements to identify time frames when adoption success is measured and approval is sought.

- Specify the change management activities that are carried out in the project as opposed to the program.

- Identify the lead and the respective roles of the project manager and program manager; provide reporting relationships/coordination points, when applicable.

6.3.1.6 Begin Change Communication

Early on, invite stakeholders to raise questions and concerns regarding the project, identify a place/individual to address these concerns, and determine a process for reviewing and responding to these questions and concerns.

Denial and fear are two primary forms of resistance to a change effort. Denial occurs when people do not believe the change will take place and may result in a change of project requirements later on. Use focus groups and interviews to allow stakeholders to discuss what would change and how it would impact the work environment.

Fear of change can lead to a stubborn insistence on the status quo, and if not explored, may impede project progress.

6.3.2 Plan Change

Planning for change management activities may be performed as part of the program or may be shared responsibilities of the program and project managers. The steps for planning change management center around project scheduling, risk management, and stakeholder engagement with special considerations to process steps in Sections 6.3.2.1 through 6.3.2.3.

6.3.2.1 Define the Change Approach

- **Collect change management requirements.** In addition to requirements identified in the *PMBOK® Guide*, consider change readiness assessment, change management scope, and change management coordination between program and project management. Identify the following:
  - o Process design/redesign requirements, including the level of complexity and/or interaction with other processes and required expertise;

- o Organizational design requirements (staffing, reporting relationships, organizational structures, policies, procedures, and required expertise);

- o Skills and abilities requirements;

- o Communications;

- o Stakeholder interests;

- o Benefits requirements (acceptance, adoption, and sustainability of the change); and

- o Cultural requirements (attitudes, political agendas, external influences, etc., affecting adoption or sustainability of the change).

As highlighted in Section 5, the purpose of requirements collection from a change management perspective is to *expand* the project team's knowledge of all potential needs and impediments. Requirements gathering is most effective when the greatest number of impacted people are involved in this activity.

Many of the same tools and techniques described in Section 5.2.2 of the *PMBOK® Guide* – Fifth Edition are appropriate for use in obtaining requirements pertinent to change management. Once gathered, these requirements may be indicative of more adaptive changes to the program management activities, in particular the stakeholder engagement plan or transition plan. As with any other changes to project/ program plans, signoff from stakeholders is important for any changes to plans generated from change management requirements.

- **Define, sequence, resource, and budget change management activities.** Apply critical skills to change management, for example, creating work breakdown structures, scheduling, resource planning, and budgeting are all critical skills to be applied to change management as well.

  - o Coordinate resource planning effectively, because it is often extensive when large and multiple groups of stakeholders are involved;

  - o Use experienced facilitators when large or multiple stakeholder groups are involved (may have procurement and budget implications when expertise does not exist in the organization);

  - o Develop organization-wide standard templates and tools for change management requirements collection to stimulate thinking, reduce time, and provide an orderly approach to change management; and

  - o Outline, sequence, and resource activities needed to transition the change into business operations. (Consider using additional steps, such as testing out new processes to support the change, verifying that policy changes have been well communicated, etc.).

Change management activities are best managed when fully integrated into a project's schedule, as illustrated in Figure 6-2. (For ease of illustration, this schedule depicts a project that is not part of a program and assumes accountability for all change management activities.)

- **Identify measures of benefits realization.** Although benefits realization is part of program management, project managers operating with a change management mindset are aware of how well the project is tracking toward the delivery of benefits. It is helpful to think of benefits realization measures along a spectrum on two paths as shown in Figure 6-3.

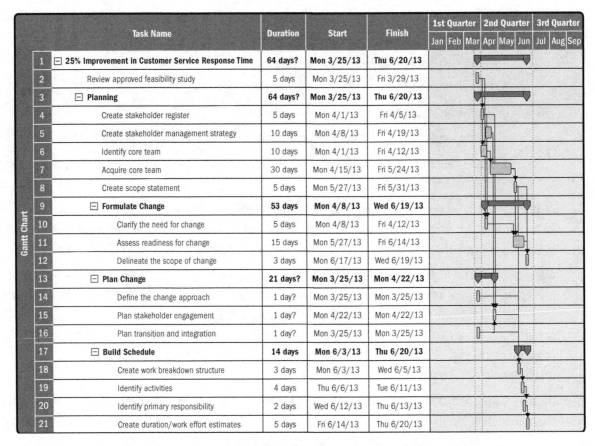

	Task Name	Duration	Start	Finish	1st Quarter	2nd Quarter	3rd Quarter
					Jan Feb Mar	Apr May Jun	Jul Aug Sep
1	⊟ 25% Improvement in Customer Service Response Time	64 days?	Mon 3/25/13	Thu 6/20/13			
2	Review approved feasibility study	5 days	Mon 3/25/13	Fri 3/29/13			
3	⊟ Planning	64 days?	Mon 3/25/13	Thu 6/20/13			
4	Create stakeholder register	5 days	Mon 4/1/13	Fri 4/5/13			
5	Create stakeholder management strategy	10 days	Mon 4/8/13	Fri 4/19/13			
6	Identify core team	10 days	Mon 4/1/13	Fri 4/12/13			
7	Acquire core team	30 days	Mon 4/15/13	Fri 5/24/13			
8	Create scope statement	5 days	Mon 5/27/13	Fri 5/31/13			
9	⊟ Formulate Change	53 days	Mon 4/8/13	Wed 6/19/13			
10	Clarify the need for change	5 days	Mon 4/8/13	Fri 4/12/13			
11	Assess readiness for change	15 days	Mon 5/27/13	Fri 6/14/13			
12	Delineate the scope of change	3 days	Mon 6/17/13	Wed 6/19/13			
13	⊟ Plan Change	21 days?	Mon 3/25/13	Mon 4/22/13			
14	Define the change approach	1 day?	Mon 3/25/13	Mon 3/25/13			
15	Plan stakeholder engagement	1 day?	Mon 4/22/13	Mon 4/22/13			
16	Plan transition and integration	1 day?	Mon 3/25/13	Mon 3/25/13			
17	⊟ Build Schedule	14 days	Mon 6/3/13	Thu 6/20/13			
18	Create work breakdown structure	3 days	Mon 6/3/13	Wed 6/5/13			
19	Identify activities	4 days	Thu 6/6/13	Tue 6/11/13			
20	Identify primary responsibility	2 days	Wed 6/12/13	Thu 6/13/13			
21	Create duration/work effort estimates	5 days	Fri 6/14/13	Thu 6/20/13			

Figure 6-2. Change Management Activities Integrated into a Project Schedule

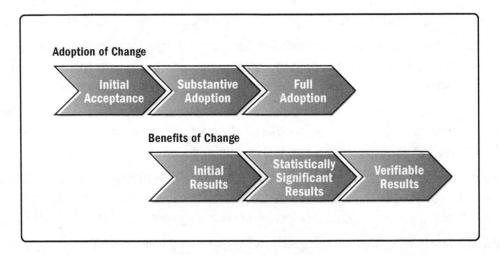

Figure 6-3. Delivery of Benefits

The adoption rate of the change is a leading indicator for obtaining the desired results. One important activity in change management is to ensure that there are organizationally sound measurement systems, targets, and resources in place to continue operational measurement of full adoption of the change and resulting outcomes over time. When a project is not part of a program, the planning for operational measurement becomes the responsibility of the project team.

Benefits mapping and benefits registers are useful tools for visualizing planned benefits and tracking the measures that will be assessed. These measures may be qualitative and quantitative and should address:

- Acceptance rates (how quickly and what percentage of people are working to achieve the change versus those who are against it and are not doing anything);
- Adoption rates (how quickly and how many are achieving proficiency to perform in the changed environment);
- Project outcomes (what is the acceptable rate for movement from a baseline state to a target state); and
- Assumptions (which tests are being used to determine the validity of assumptions).

- **Clarify risks to change acceptance, adoption, and realization, and plan abatement activities.** Change management risks tend to be in areas where there is an inability to achieve or absorb all the benefits, or where there are changes to the contextual environment for the change. Risks for achieving change benefits fall into several categories.

  - People risks (e.g., forms of resistance to change, political agendas, competition for power, and fear of loss of status or job);
  - Cultural risks (e.g., risk avoidance, group think, policies, or norms (unwritten guides to behavior) that contraindicate the change, control culture, unclear decision-making paths, or norms);
  - Capability development risks (e.g., insufficient training and learning reinforcement, inability to respond to questions/problems, low starting capability or capacity, poor methods for institutionalizing learning, withholding/protecting knowledge, lack of informal learning);
  - Process development risks (e.g., insufficient employee involvement in process definition, processes dominated by single-skilled people, lack of experience with process development tools, work decisions only made at high levels);
  - Organizational structure/management risks (e.g., weak leadership, too many layers of management, dispersed decision-making authority, matrix management, unclear role definitions);
  - Time risks (e.g., unacceptable time frames for absorption of change, competing time priorities of resources needed for the project (training, process design, etc.); and
  - Environmental risks (e.g., market volatility, changing competition, changing technology, changing leadership, regulatory or legal uncertainty, inability to absorb magnitude of change).

When planning for risk, identify the means for assessing/measuring whether risks are materializing, the events or levels of risk that will trigger responses in the risk mitigation plan, and the schedule for a formalized assessment of emerging risks. Risk mitigation activities that are most useful in change management include those shown in Table 6-4.

Table 6-4. Typical Risk Mitigation Activities in Change Management

Change Management Area	Risk Abatement Activity
Communication	• Repetition of messages regarding need for change and vision for future • More frequent and/or targeted communication of status, facts, milestones, issues and solutions, changing assumptions or environment
Feedback	• More frequent, widespread, or intense requests for input • More brainstorming and innovation-seeking techniques • More invitations for opposing points of view • More delegated decision making
Development	• More targeted or intense training • More simulation and practice • Additional mentors, coaches, and early experts • Additional outside expertise • Additional methods for learning from each other
Energy	• Management modeling of new behaviors • Renewed/intensified leadership enthusiasm and support • Involvement of early adopters in aiding acceptance • Celebrations of early successes • Public appreciation for work being done

6.3.2.2 Plan Stakeholder Engagement

In a large-scale change effort, use separate plans to cover key areas such as communication activities, human resources activities (organizational design, training, etc.), and process development activities. Although these plans will be coordinated by the program manager, Annex A1 of the *PMBOK® Guide* emphasizes that projects should use "appropriate management strategies to effectively engage stakeholders throughout the project life cycle, based on the analysis of their needs, interests, and potential impact on project success."

The stakeholder management plan (more appropriately seen as a stakeholder engagement plan in change management) incorporates advance planning for communications, but is also designed to identify needed communications based on the occurrence of risks identified in the risk register. The stakeholder management plan addresses key players and messages, and makes extensive use of the change readiness assessment, assumptions uncovered during requirements definition, and the risk register when defining both proactive and adaptive/reactive actions.

With regard to change management issues, the stakeholder management plan should inform; create ownership and distribute decision making; explore and grow important relationships among stakeholders; invite and share relevant knowledge and experience; build confidence and competence; identify and address issues, concerns, and resistance; and reinforce successful movement to the future state.

The plan should clearly spell out the responsibilities, timelines, and adaptive responsibilities for sponsors, program manager, lead, integrator, project manager, operational leadership, and external partners.

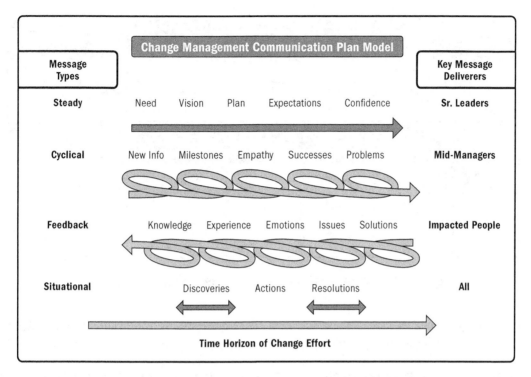

Figure 6-4. Communications Management Plan Model

Refer to the model communications management plan in Figure 6-4 that covers several concurrent spectrums of communication activities.

- Steady messaging is planned messaging that keeps goals, plans, and expectations highlighted; it is most often more top-down messaging.

- Cyclical messaging offers real-time updates during the course of change. Though planned in timing and methods, the content of the messaging responds to new information, such as issues or successes, and offers both facts and emotional support. Messaging is best delivered by the manager in close proximity to those impacted; therefore, there may be multiple variations of cyclical messaging strategies.

- Feedback is also a planned and continuing messaging strategy during change. Information is solicited from employees and that information serves as an input to adaptive changes in the program and/or project management plan, which may trigger risk responses.

- Situational messages are bursts of information, used when something new is discovered or an issue is uncovered and resolved.

Use multiple or varied approaches in the stakeholder management plan, depending upon the needs of the audience. For example, what is communicated, how often, and by whom is different for early adapters than for those who want to wait and see how the change works; monitoring-and-response activities may need to be more

Defining Process Group						
	Information	Ownership	Knowledge	Competence	Issues	Reinforcement
When/who	Action	Action	Action	Action	Action	Action
When/who	Action	Action	Action	Action	Action	Action
When/who	Action	Action	Action	Action	Action	Action
Adaptive Activities						
	Information	Ownership	Knowledge	Competence	Issues	Reinforcement
Trigger/Measure and Timing	Action	Action	Action	Action	Action	Action
Trigger/Measure and Timing	Action	Action	Action	Action	Action	Action
Trigger/Measure and Timing	Action	Action	Action	Action	Action	Action

Figure 6-5. Sample Engagement/Communication Plan Structure

frequent and thorough for change-averse stakeholders than for those who welcome change; engagement planning may need to secure early buy-in of those who can influence others.

Structure the stakeholder management plan content using a template (see example shown in Figure 6-5).

6.3.2.3 Plan Transition and Integration

Consider the actions and work activities needed to effectively transition the project outcomes into normal business operations when not included in the program management plan. The *PMBOK® Guide* identifies the need to plan for closeout activities to include "actions and activities necessary to transfer the project's products, services, or results to the next phase or to production and/or operations." There are three categories of activities that are useful to consider and build into a project's transition plan as appropriate:

- Volume and size transition (moving from a pilot, sample, or test environment to a fully operational environment);

- Capability and expertise transition (moving from an expert-driven set of capabilities to broad capability in all processes, including management processes required for the change);

- Managerial transition (moving from a project-managed and sponsor-driven environment to an operations-managed and operations-driven environment, using normal business management processes for hiring/training, for measurement of work effectiveness, and supervisory oversight, etc.).

6.3.3 Implement Change Process

Project implementation and change implementation are similar in that the project manager ensures that the change management aspects of the project are monitored against the schedule, resource requirements, and budget established in the project management plan. Risk responses are more iterative and may need to be readjusted more frequently than in a typical project.

6.3.3.1 Prepare Organization for Change

Implementing change requires activities that are foundational and preparatory for activities to implement the change. These preparatory activities assure that resources are aligned to propel the change effort. In many cases, these activities are coordinated through program management.

Activities related to preparing for implementation may be coordinated through a designated change management team. The change management team may be an extended project team or part of a larger program management team. Change management resources supplied by the organization or procured externally include, but are not limited to:

- Training resources (e.g., training, mentoring, and testing);
- Communications resources (e.g., surveying, influencing, and issue organization and response);
- Process design resources (e.g., process development/mapping, specifications, simulating, and testing);
- Human resources (e.g., facilitating groups and addressing behavioral problems during change);
- Benefits measurement expertise (e.g., benefits mapping and benefits register development);
- Organizational design (e.g., job descriptions, staff planning, leadership development, and organizational structure design); and
- Cultural assessment and development expertise (e.g., development of normative behaviors and policies).

6.3.3.2 Mobilize Stakeholders

Consider mobilizing stakeholders, purposefully and continuously, as the most important aspect of implementing change other than defining clear measures of success. As such, this activity requires constant monitoring and adaptation during the course of implementation and socialization of the change. While all activities and resources of a project are managed, perhaps none are as important to the successful integration of change as managing communications and engagement. It is one of the most dynamic aspects of the plan, requiring continual review and adaptation during execution of the project. The communications management plan responds to the many environmental or contextual shifts that occur during the project, including:

- Resistance to or acceptance of a change that is greater than anticipated or comes from unanticipated sources, etc.;
- Unforeseen transition or integration issues;
- Unforeseen conflicts among people/groups related to the change;
- Challenge or unsuitability of project outputs due to changing circumstances, sponsor pressure, apathy, or missteps;
- Changing management support for the effort; and
- Changes in the assumptions that are the basis for anticipated outcomes.

Effective change communications include proactive steps to periodically assess the degree of acceptance for the change. Such assessments can unearth issues before they build or inflict greater damage. For example,

Table 6-5. Project Control in Change Management

Project Control Options	When is a Change Management Option Important?
Change scope	• When an assumption that is critical to realizing the benefits of a project is inaccurate, especially when it affects future results in the program • When a change in a contextual factor significantly changes the ability to realize the benefits of a project, but still allows the project to contribute to the ultimate outcomes • When a deliverable is no longer needed
Defer scope elements to another project	• When an assumption that is not critical to realizing the benefits of a project is inaccurate and will not significantly affect future results • When a change in a contextual factor can be accommodated at another time without impacting timeliness of the outcomes
Extend schedule	• When additional stakeholders are identified whose influence could derail the change effort • When additional people are impacted by the project and their capacity to operate in the changed environment is important to realize benefits • When transition is more difficult than initially planned
Add resources/budget	• When additional people are impacted by the project and their capacity to operate in the changed environment is important to realize benefits
Stop project	• When a change in a contextual factor fundamentally changes the ability to achieve the ultimate outcome

these assessments may uncover (a) misinformation that is filtering through the organization, (b) conflicts that are developing, or (c) unanticipated opposing views that can be addressed or unanticipated supportive influences that can be enhanced.

6.3.3.3 Deliver Project Outputs

In the context of a change effort, delivering the actual project outputs requires continuous monitoring and project management plan modifications to optimize planned benefits.

- **Assess change progress.** In addition to tracking project scope, schedule, and budget, success requires that project progress also be measured against the leading indicators for benefit realization. Report these measures to sponsors, and when appropriate, to the program manager, as part of project reporting.

- **Review and modify, as appropriate, scope, activities, schedule, and budget.** Understanding that change is the fluid environment in which a project occurs, address issues that arise during change efforts in the project scope, schedule, and resource control. Change management is useful in evaluating how to address challenges to the change effort (see Table 6-5). Considering the impact of risk realization on the intended outcomes in the benefits register allows project managers to select the most appropriate project control responses.

6.3.4 Manage Transition

The transition of a project's deliverables into business operations is planned at the project level (see 6.3.2.3) and may be supported by activities planned as part of program management. *The Standard for Program Management –*

Third Edition highlights the need for a project to address "the need for ongoing activities such as product support, service management, change management, user engagement, or customer support from a program component to an operational support function in order for the ongoing benefits to be achieved."

6.3.4.1 Transition Outputs into Business

Project outputs do not necessarily translate to an effective operational capacity for the change. A project output becomes operationally effective when:

- An acceptable number of people adopt it and use it effectively in day-to-day operations after project completion.
- Management systems are in place to ensure the effective performance of the new work activity at acceptable levels of performance.
- Measures and goals are established to ensure viability of the new processes and their operational effectiveness.
- Support systems are in place to provide assistance in the performance of changed work.
- People performing the changed work have a means to voice and elicit responses to issues and new ideas or opportunities to enhance the benefits of the products or services.

The project team completes a plan for ensuring that benefits are sustained over the course of time. Sustainability plans typically consider:

- Work performance measures that will be tracked, baselines that need to be improved, and timelines for improving work performance;
- Training updates or added capability development (e.g., better use of specific elements of a new system);
- Method for identifying and responding to issues or problems;
- Periodic assessments to ensure adoption and usage rates of the changed environment continue to advance;
- Periodic assessments of progress on transitions between work groups or processes; and
- Review of new ideas or improvements offered for the changed environment (a key indicator of adoption and usage).

6.3.4.2 Measure Adoption Rate and Outcomes/Benefits

Some practices to assure benefits realization occur throughout the project, many toward the end of implementation, and others after deliverables and before project closeout. Some practices carry through all of these points in time.

During transition into operations, it is particularly important to continue to measure adoption rates and evidence of results in order to form baselines from which more complete benefits realization and operational standards can be measured over time. The following measures can be used to judge the adoption, adaptation, and ultimate benefits realization of the change effort.

- **Conduct acceptance/adoption assessments.** During the course of a change effort, assess emotional states, in order to adjust interventional activities like training or communication. Apply both quantitative and qualitative techniques to these assessments, to determine the degree of acceptance and how it changes over time, in addition to what is working and what impediments still remain.

  Acceptance levels vary: when new information is shared and the vision becomes more real, it often results in a dip in enthusiasm and increased skepticism; when the change is in progress, frustration and fear of failure surface. Generally, as the implementation project moves forward, acceptance levels show steadier increases. An acceptance assessment finding of continued negativity well into implementation may reflect either a fatal flaw in the selected solution or a confusing or incomplete implementation plan.

  It is crucial to benefits realization that the change be adopted and people operate as planned/visioned in the changed environment. Perform assessments throughout the life of the project, and share results with all affected people, along with requests for suggestions. Build a historical view of acceptance levels and types of problems that surface along the course of a change effort to reassure and inform those affected, and provide predictability to future change efforts.

- **Measure benefits realization against established measures and address variances.** An adopted change may not realize intended benefits due to faulty assumptions, overly optimistic outcomes measures, or other factors. Change efforts are incremental; therefore, when benefit realization is incomplete in one increment, the achievement of the full range of benefits in subsequent efforts may be challenged.

  Benefits measures, baselines, targets, and measurement periods/frequencies are outlined in the benefits register during planning, and measurement activities are performed when the changes are implemented and adopted, extending beyond project closeout, most often in program management when the project deliverables are transitioned into the business. Benefits registers are reviewed to clarify appropriate actions. Many of these actions are performed at the program management level when the project is part of a program and include, but are not limited to:

  o Change assumptions in subsequent iterations of the change effort;

  o Modify time frames for achieving full benefits realization and update benefits register;

  o Change expectations of outcomes in subsequent phases and add phases when necessary;

  o Change timing of subsequent phases;

  o Identify risks for subsequent phases; and

  o Discontinue change effort, when agreed upon.

6.3.5 Sustain Change

Section 6.3.4 covered the activities required to move through the process of change, taking into consideration what people need in order to change in a way that will maximize the intended benefits of the change. However, in order to successfully implement change, it is crucial to repeat and emphasize the activities that are concurrent with and crucially adjunct to traditional project management activities.

6.3.5.1 Ongoing Consultation and Representation of Stakeholders

As discussed in Section 2, stakeholder input, involvement, and mobilization toward change goals are the most crucial goals of change management. Ongoing consultation and representation of stakeholders is achieved through:

- Involvement in the definition of the vision for the change, the extent of the change to achieve the vision, and the identification of impediments to the change;
- Involvement in decision making during the course of the change effort by delegating authority for decisions to those most directly affected to the maximum extent possible;
- Mobilizing stakeholders in the implementation processes (e.g., process design, organization design, training/mentoring, and facilities design, etc.);
- Seeking and using stakeholder input in assessing acceptance, adoption, and initial results of the change effort; and
- Seeking and using stakeholder suggestions to optimize the benefits of the change.

6.3.5.2 Conduct Sensemaking Activities

As described in Section 5.3.5.2, sensemaking activities are those activities undertaken throughout the program and project to create a common understanding of the change effort's goals, intended outcomes, impacts, and implementation process.

Sensemaking activities in project management occur mainly through the planned actions defined in the stakeholder management plan. However, sensemaking also occurs through informal channels, so project managers need to assess how well these informal sensemaking efforts adhere to and benefit the change effort. When informal methods contribute more to confusion than to support, risk mitigation actions are necessary.

6.3.5.3 Measure Benefits Realization

The process of measuring benefits realization starts during the planning process and is a constant source of attention for project managers throughout the implementation of the change and the transition of outcomes into business operations. The role of project management in benefits realization is the routine and rigorous measurement of early indicators of change success: acceptance, adoption, and early results of the change and its benefits. The integrated measurement of benefits realization is the responsibility of program management when the project is part of a larger program.

6.4 Summary

Change management in the project management context extends and reinforces the emphasis on processes, skills, tools, and techniques to achieve intended benefits of the project, program, and the organizational strategy by the following:

- Provide sufficient resources (e.g., time, people, and budget, etc.) to support and reinforce the project deliverables, including such systems as process design, organizational design, policy or procedure development, and culture change, etc.;

- Actively engage people who are interested in and/or impacted by the change in order to ensure the most complete and adoptable solution;

- Prepare for and respond to the risks of resistance or lack of acceptance of a change through well-crafted stakeholder management and communication management plans, and attentive monitoring of the signals of resistance or apathy;

- Build flexibility into project management plans to allow for the emergence of needs for adaptive changes to both the project management plan and potentially to the program management plan;

- Plan for and assess the progress of acceptance and adoption of the changes represented by the project deliverables;

- Reinforce the sustainability of the intended benefits for the change through well-planned and measurable activities to transition project deliverables into operations; and

- Perform careful and close coordination of change management interests for the project and the program.

REFERENCES

[1] Schaffer R. H., & Thomson H. A. (1992). Successful change programmes begin with results. *Harvard Business Review, 70* (1), 80–89.

[2] Project Management Institute. (2012). *Pulse of the Profession™ In-Depth Report: Organizational Agility.* Available from http://www.pmi.org/~/media/PDF/Research/ Organizational-Agility-In-Depth-Report.ashx

[3] Project Management Institute. (2013). *A Guide to the Project Management Body of Knowledge (PMBOK® Guide)* – Fifth Edition. Newtown Square, PA: PMI.

[4] Project Management Institute. (2013). *The Standard for Program Management* – Third Edition. Newtown Square, PA: PMI.

[5] Project Management Institute. (2013). *The Standard for Portfolio Management* – Third Edition. Newtown Square, PA: PMI.

[6] Project Management Institute. (2013). *Organizational Project Management Maturity Model* –Third Edition. Newtown Square, PA: PMI.

[7] Crawford L, Cooke-Davies T. (2012) *Best Industry Outcomes.* Newtown Square, PA: Project Management Institute.

[8] Project Management Institute. (2012). *Pulse of the Profession™ In Depth Report: Driving Success in Challenging Times.* Available from http://www.pmi.org/~/media/PDF/Research/2012_Pulse_of_the_profession.ashx

[9] Project Management Institute. (2013). *Pulse of the Profession™ In Depth Report: The High Cost of Low Performance.* Available from http://www.pmi.org/Business-Solutions/Pulse.aspx

[10] Watzlawick P., Weakland J. H., and Fisch R. (1974). *Change: Principles of Problem Formation and Problem Resolution.* New York: Norton, 1974.

[11] Casey, W. (2000). *Project Tools for Leading Organizational Change.* Wheat Ridge, CO: Executive Leadership Group Inc.

APPENDIX X1
CONTRIBUTORS AND REVIEWERS OF *MANAGING CHANGE IN ORGANIZATIONS: A PRACTICE GUIDE*

The Project Management Institute is grateful to all of these individuals for their support and acknowledges their contributions to the project management profession.

X1.1 Core Committee

The following individuals served as members, were contributors of text or concepts, or served as leaders within the Project Core Committee:

Claudia M. Baca, Chair, PMP, OPM Professional Services

Margaret W. Combe

Terence J. Cooke-Davies, PhD, FCMI

Stephen Garfein, MBA, PMP

Nicholas F. Horney, PhD

Marvin R. Nelson, MBA, CAE

Michel Thiry, PhD, PMI Fellow

Stephen A. Townsend

Kristin L. Vitello, CAPM, Standards Project Specialist

X1.2 Content Reviewers

In addition to the members of the Committee, the following individuals provided their review and recommendations on the draft of the practice guide:

Shyamprakash K. Agrawal, PMP, PgMP

Larry Bull

Karan Froom, CCMP

Patti Harter, PMP

Vered Holzmann, PhD., PMP

Thomas Luke Jarocki

Ginger Levin, PhD, PMP, PgMP

Robert L. Payne, PMP, PgMP

David W. Power, PMI-RMP, PMP

Shankar Sankaran, PhD, PMP

Jen L. Skrabak, MBA, PMP

Chan Keen Soon, PMP, PgMP

Richard Vann

X1.3 PMI Standards Program Member Advisory Group (MAG)

The following individuals served as members of the PMI Standards Program Member Advisory Group during development of the *Practice Guide for Managing Change in Organizations:*

Monique Aubry, PhD, MPM

Margareth Fabiola dos Santos Carneiro, MSc, PMP

Larry Goldsmith MBA, PMP

Cynthia Snyder, MBA, PMP

Chris Stevens, PhD

Dave Violette, MPM, PMP

John Zlockie, MBA, PMP, PMI Standards Manager

X1.4 Production Staff

Special mention is due to the following employees of PMI:

Donn Greenberg, Manager, Publications

Roberta Storer, Product Editor

Barbara Walsh, Publications Production Supervisor

GLOSSARY

Agent. Active proponent(s) and driver(s) of the change.

Benefits Breakdown Structure. A variation of the benefits map built on the same principles as a work breakdown structure (WBS) and using a how–why logic to link the different levels of benefits from strategic to operational.

Benefits Map. A hierarchical representation of the expected benefits of a program, classified from strategic level to operational level by linking each level using a means–end relationship.

Benefits Realization. The successful integration of the change into business as usual.

Benefits Realization Plan. A document that specifies the activities necessary for achieving the portfolio's, program's and/or project's planned benefits and specifies the mechanisms that should be in place to ensure that benefits are fully realized over time.

Business Impact Analysis. The collection of results data from programs and projects, which is fed back into the portfolio. From these results, the impact on the business is then determined.

Business Value. A concept that is unique to each organization, which includes tangible and intangible elements. Through the effective use of portfolio, program, and project management disciplines, organizations will possess the ability to employ reliable, established processes to meet enterprise objectives and obtain great business value from their investments.

Change Life Cycle Framework. A concurrent set of subprocesses where multiple activities take place in an ordered but nonsequential way. It is an iterative model where adaptive change occurs on a continual basis in response to evolving circumstances.

Change Management. A comprehensive, cyclic, and structured approach for transitioning individuals, groups, and organizations from a current state to a future state with intended business benefits.

Change Readiness Assessment. A measure of the reality of the current organization in relation to the future state from two perspectives: organizational systems and structures that need to be improved or will support the change; and the people and culture that are able to support or may resist the change.

Critical Success Factor. The high-level objectives of the portfolio, program, or project and the contributing enablers that are required to be in place to ensure outcomes.

Culture. An explicit way of working (the formal systems and processes in place and how they operate) and a tacit level of operation (the informal and semiformal networks and other activities people employ to get things done and bypass, subvert, or seek to influence the more formal processes). Culture is generally thought of as "the way we do things around here."

Current State. The "as-is" state of the organization prior to the initiation of a new portfolio, program, or project.

Enterprise Environmental Factors. Conditions, not under the immediate control of the team, that influence, constrain, or direct the portfolio, program, or project.

Future State. The "to-be" state of the organization after the completion of a new portfolio, program, or project.

Governance Board. A review and decision-making body responsible for approving and supporting recommendations made by the program(s) under its authority, and for monitoring and managing the progress of such program(s) in achieving the stated goals.

Integrator. The integrator function is responsible for the preparation and integration of the change into the business.

Key Performance Indicators. Measurable performance indicators for each of the objectives of the portfolio, program, or project, which demonstrate benefits realization.

Lead. The lead function supports the overall change management process and implementation including coordination of associated work streams within the scope of the project.

Organizational Agility. See *strategic agility*.

Organizational Enablers. Organizational enablers are structural, cultural, technological, and human-resource practices that can be leveraged to support the implementation of Best Practices in portfolios, programs, and projects in support of strategic goals.

Organizational Environment. The policies and supporting practices of the organization that are created to support the OPM strategy execution framework and delivery of the organization's strategy.

Organizational Process Assets. Plans, processes, policies, procedures, and knowledge bases specific to and used by the performing organization.

Organizational Project Management (OPM). The application of knowledge, skills, tools, and techniques to organizational activities and portfolio, program, and project activities to achieve the aims of an organization through projects.

Organizational Project Management Maturity Model (*OPM3®*). A framework that defines knowledge, assessment, and improvement processes, based on Best Practices and Capabilities, to help organizations measure and mature their portfolio, program, and project management practices.

Portfolio. Projects, programs, subportfolios, and operations managed as a group to achieve strategic objectives.

Portfolio Management. The centralized management of one or more portfolios to achieve strategic objectives.

Portfolio Process Assets. Portfolio plans, processes, policies, procedures, and knowledge bases used by the portfolio manager and stakeholders.

Program. A group of related projects, subprograms, and program activities that are managed in a coordinated way to obtain benefits not available from managing them individually.

Program Management. The application of knowledge, skills, tools, and techniques to a program to meet the program requirements and to obtain benefits and control not available by managing projects individually.

Project. A temporary endeavor undertaken to create a unique product, service, or result.

Project Management. The application of knowledge, skills, tools, and techniques to project activities to meet the project requirements.

Project Management Knowledge Areas. An identified area of project management defined by its knowledge requirements and described in terms of its component processes, practices, inputs, outputs, tools, and techniques.

Project Management Process Groups. A logical grouping of project management inputs, tools and techniques, and outputs. The Project Management Process Groups include initiating processes, planning processes, executing processes, monitoring and controlling processes, and closing processes. Project Management Process Groups are not project phases.

Recipient. A person directly or indirectly impacted by a change.

Sensemaking. The conversational and social practices that enable individuals and groups to make sense of what is happening around them

Sponsor. A person or group who provides resources and support for the project, program, or portfolio, and is accountable for enabling success.

Stakeholder. An individual, group, or organization who may affect, be affected by, or perceive itself to be affected by a decision, activity, or outcome of a project, program, or portfolio.

Stakeholder Analysis. A technique of systematically gathering and analyzing quantitative and qualitative information to determine whose interests should be taken into account throughout the project.

Stakeholder Management Plan. The stakeholder management plan is a subsidiary plan of the project management plan that defines the processes, procedures, tools, and techniques to effectively engage stakeholders in project decisions and execution based on the analyis of their needs, interests, and potential impact.

Strategic Agility. Strategic agility is defined as the capability of a business to proactively seize and take advantage of business environment changes while demonstrating resilience resulting from unforeseen changes.

Value Performance Analysis. Providing business value realization data from value business fulfillment back to the strategy of the organization.

INDEX

A

Adaptive change, 66, 84
    in addressing discrepancies, 85–86
    in change life cycle framework, 20
    in change life cycle framework–project, 96
    in change life cycles–program, 68, 90
    in coordination of program, project, and change processes, 97
    in managing transition, 83
Agents, 39, 83
    description, 11
    sensemaking and, 88
    stakeholder mobilization and, 80, 82
AHP. *See* Analytic Hierarchical Process
Analytic Hierarchical Process (AHP), 71

B

Barriers, potential, 36–39
Benefits, 34, 93
    breakdown structure, 73
    delivery of, 90, 97, 104
    measure, 61–63, 84–85, 88–89, 103–105, 111–113
    non-financial, 75
Benefits realization, 61–63, 88–89, 103–105
Bureaucracy, 38

C

Case studies, 59
Change
    cycles of, 29–30
    formulating, 18–20
    focus for initiative, 33–35
    implementing, 18, 21
    managing transition of, 18, 21
    planning, 18, 20–21
    psychology of, 2, 13
    sustaining, 18, 21
Change agenda, 31

Change curve, 13–14
Change life cycle framework, 19–22
    adaptive change in, 20
    change management and, 19–21
    formulate change, 19–20
    implement change, 21
    manage transition, 21
    OPM and, 28
    plan change, 20–21
    portfolio management and, 48
    program management and, 66
    project management and, 30, 96
    sustain change, 21
Change life cycle –OPM, 28
Change life cycle framework–project, 30, 96
Change life cycle–program, 30, 66–68
Change life cycles, 67–68
    OPM, 28
    portfolio management and change management and, 29–30
    program management and, 66
    project management and, 30, 96
Change management
    activities in Project Management Process Groups, 98
    change as strategy, 9
    change life cycle framework, 19–21
    corporate culture in, 18–19
    critical factors impede or foster change, 22
    developing agile culture, 10
    external drivers of change, 9–10
    nature and process of change, 12–19
        common models of change, 12–18
    OPM and, 23–41
    overview, 7–9
    portfolio and, 43–64
    program and, 65–92
    project and, 93–114
    sponsoring change, 10–12

Process improvement, 16
Program life cycle
    change life cycles and, 68, 90
    change management life cycle and, 66–68
    phases of, 97
Program management, 25
    change life cycles and, 30, 66–68, 90, 97
    nature and process of change, 12
    OPM and, 28–29
Program management and change management,
        65–92
    change management practices in, 68–90
        formulate change, 69–75
        implement change, 80–83
        manage transition, 83–86
        plan change, 75–80
        sustain change, 86–89
    context of, 65–68
        application of, 67–68
        program and change life cycles, 66–68
        program management definition, 66–67
        program management standard, 67
    organizational capabilities, 91
    overview, 65
    summary, 92
Project charter, 98–99
Project management
    change life cycles and, 30
    nature and process of change, 12
Project management and change management, 93–114
    context, 93–97
        application, 96–97
        Knowledge Areas, 97, 99
        Process Groups, 96–97
    overview, 93
    practices, 97–113
        begin change communication, 102
        conduct sensemaking activities, 113
        define change approach, 102–106
        deliver project outputs, 110
        implement change process, 108
        manage transition, 110–111
        measure adoption rate and outcomes/benefits,
            111–112
        measure benefits realization, 113
        mobilize stakeholders, 109–110

        ongoing stakeholders' consultation and
            representation, 113
        plan change, 102–108
        plan stakeholder engagement, 106–108
        plan transition and integration, 108
        prepare organization for change, 109
        sustain change, 112–113
        transition outputs into business, 111
    summary, 114
Project management information system (PMIS), 72
Proportional voting, 74
Psychological transition, 2, 13–14, 94–95

R

Readiness
    assessment of, 31–32, 51, 54–61, 71–72
    failure to build, 38
    sponsors and, 41
    time and, 72
    urgency versus, 50–52
Recipients, 11–12
    category of change and, 16–17
    mobilization of, 82–83
Research, 26–27
Risk mitigation, 105–106
Roadmap
    delineate scope, 73, 75
    elements of, 78

S

Scope delineation, 72–75
Sensemaking activities, 87–88, 113
Simple rating system, 74
Soft systems analysis, 71
Sponsors, 11
    capabilities of, 37, 40–41
    initiative focus, 33–34
    issues, 41
    readiness, 41
Stakeholders, 13–14, 77
    communication and, 87
    corporate culture and, 19
    engagement plan for, 79
    map, 69–70